Your Moment
to Lead

There are all types of leaders and leadership styles. Some lead from the front and are charismatic although not necessarily overly humble! One of the greatest leaders in history, Jesus Christ, had the balance right. Forthright, empathetic, judicious but compassionate and merciful. This type of leadership attracts. People connect. That is Jacob. People are attracted to his sincere and innate ability to connect "in the moment." When it is time to stand up, he is there – leadership in the moment. The trust this engenders is what will inspire people who read this book to listen and follow.

Will Wilson
40 years in legal and project leadership roles

Your Moment to Lead

Simple But Important Ways to
Prepare for Leadership

JACOB ISAAC

Your Moment to Lead
Published by Jacob Isaac
with Castle Publishing Ltd
New Zealand

jakeisaacdaily@gmail.com

© 2023 Jacob Isaac

ISBN 978-0-473-66956-0 (Softcover)
ISBN 978-0-473-66957-7 (ePUB)
ISBN 978-0-473-66958-4 (Kindle)

Editing:
Rachel Ross

Production & Typesetting:
Andrew Killick
Castle Publishing Services
www.castlepublishing.co.nz

Cover Design:
Paul Smith

ALL RIGHTS RESERVED

No part of this publication may be reproduced, stored in a retrieval system, or transmitted in any form or by any means, electronic, mechanical, photocopying, recording or otherwise, without prior written permission from the author.

Forewords

As a consultant, coach and author, I have been asked to define the essence of a world-class leader. Usually, I would fall back on the most straightforward answer given by John Maxwell, the *New York Times* bestselling author. He says, "Leadership is influence. Always has been and always will be."

While this definition by John Maxwell is simple and broad, it points to the reality that leadership exists in every organization at every level. Why? Because influence exists at every level. Some influence is for good and some, well... not so good.

Jacob Isaac's latest book, *Your Moment to Lead*, is a step-by-step guide for taking control of your leadership reputation and influencing for good. In ten chapters, he gives you a roadmap for growing your leadership reputation, no matter where you sit in the organization.

What Jacob shares with you in the pages of this book is not just theory. It is an applied approach, and by that, I mean you will not only get the tools, but you will also get the wisdom of his personal experience in using them.

The wisdom in the following pages will open your eyes to pursuing the essential leadership qualities of growing healthy relationships, making wise decisions, influencing with integrity, being an effective communicator, leading from a positive mindset, and leading by example.

Jacob will challenge you to step away from adopting someone else's idea of who you should be as a leader and inspire you to step up and be the leader that only you can be.

After all, we live in a time that demands authentic leadership, and this is your moment to be the influencer for good. This is your moment to lead.

Eugene Moreau
Certified Master Coach and Author

The secular business world is inundated with bosses, managers, directors, and CEOs. However, genuine leadership is lacking despite all their business qualifications and expertise. More than qualified managers, directors, etc., there is a dire need for *motivational leadership* – people who can reproduce after their kind others who are even more dynamic than themselves.

Undoubtedly, the above statement is solid and valid in that when needing new leadership, most companies import from without, which shows the lack of good leadership qualities within the company. Companies that continually import leadership from without not only do not have authentic leadership within, but they are also showing the inadequacies of their company and disrespect to the workforce, who often have served the company faithfully for several years.

Companies with a leadership development program have an ongoing successful business future because they have invested in the people who have worked diligently and have been rewarded for their loyalty and skills developed within the company.

I have known Jacob Isaac for over 35 years, watching him mature into a dynamic leader in all fields of life – a sportsman, pastor/teacher, visionary, and resolute secular worker. I say this, for I saw within Jacob the necessary qualifications for leadership as itemized below:

Perfection Versus Potential

One of the significant mistakes in choosing future leaders is the failure to realize that no one is born a leader. Leadership is developed in others by seasoned leaders, people who have proven themselves and have followers who want to emulate the leader they are following. A good leader, therefore, is someone who has the ability to turn a 'nobody' into a somebody who will evolve into a leadership role. As much as the leader will see imperfections in leadership prospects, he or she will concentrate on the strong potential of those selected to develop as future leaders.

The Acronym for Respect

R stands for respect: Considering the acronym for respect and employing the principles thereof gives the future leader the understanding that the leader training him treats him as an equal and not as an inferior.

The leader must show respect to those who train for leadership. He or she must always treat them as his or her equals. He must never talk down to them. Respect earns respect. Future leaders develop more quickly when their leader respects them.

E stands for enthuse: The leader, when teaching, must be enthusiastic. His enthusiasm acts as a firebrand that lights up a future leader's desire to become a dynamic leader.

S stands for serve: Just as parents serve their children healthy meals to develop the children's growth, similarly, the leader must serve future leaders with the appropriate teachings considering their stages of growth. Strange but true, the leader must adopt an attitude of servanthood to guide and influence potential future leaders.

P stands for praise: People respond to praise, and whenever the future leader excels, the supervisor gives him or her a good pat on the back.

E stands for encourage: Sometimes, the future leader will trip up. When this happens, a conscientious leader will not scold him or her. Instead, a dynamic leader will provide encouragement by explaining how it is possible to learn from mistakes.

C stands for congratulate: Whenever the future leader excels in assignments, he or she should be shown excitement. The supervisor should convey a sense of satisfaction and pride in what the future leader has achieved.

T stands for thanks: When the time of training is over, the new leader should be thanked by the supervisor for the honor of helping to develop the new leader's skills.

Joseph D'Allende, DipTh, BTh, D.D.

Contents

Preface		11
1.	Define Your Character	13
2.	Pursue Your Passion	33
3.	Assess Your Potential to Lead	53
4.	Build Workplace Relationships	71
5.	Be Positive	91
6.	Establish Integrity	107
7.	Communicate Effectively	123
8.	Continue to Grow	137
9.	Get Involved	151
10.	Step Up and Lead	165
Closing Thoughts		177
Endnotes		179
About the Author		184

Preface

At work or where you live, you may get opportunities to take the lead. But whether incidental or long-awaited, leadership roles don't come along every day. If you are interested in becoming a future leader, this book can show you how to start preparing naturally to seize the moment when leadership beckons. You don't need an MBA from Harvard. You can work with the interests, skills, and experience you have to become the leader you want to be.

My leadership journey began at 16 when I noticed the types of leaders around me. Educators, businesspeople, and managers influenced my life and, through their inspirational examples, left impressions on how to lead others. I can recall the seeds of leadership sown in my life with each passing year. As I developed insight and gained experience in youth, at church, on the job, in business, or at family events, people began turning to me for direction, guidance, or advice.

Today I am 58 years old with more than 40 years of leadership experience. My university education did not specifically train me to be a leader. Rather, everyday life led me through a series of experiences that formed and strengthened my potential to guide others. Organically and intuitively, my professional work shaped my lifelong interests and an aptitude to coach those who turned to me for help.

I wrote this book to share with you the processes that

impacted my early managerial tendencies. The chapters describe firsthand experiences and professional tools that prepared me to take the helm when duty called, or opportunity beckoned. Determined not to become an egotist, megalomaniac, or control freak like some I had met over the years, I followed the path of becoming a humble and helpful leader to support the needs and goals of family, friends, and colleagues as much as my own.

From organizing a project to motivating a team, I would like to offer my experience to help you discover and develop your natural leadership qualities. Leadership isn't about a commanding presence or an arrogant manner. You can lead others by simply being yourself and sharing what you have learned.

Everyone has the potential to lead. But not all will recognize the inner qualities that equip them to influence others for positive outcomes.

Are you ready to explore your natural leadership abilities and put them to beneficial use when your moment to shine appears?

Chapter 1

Define Your Character

When you think back to when you were a child growing up, do you remember what your family said about you?

"Wow, you're a great runner! You're going to become a professional athlete!"

"Would you draw another picture for the fridge? You have an amazing artistic talent for an eight-year-old."

"Look at him ride that bike – he could be a race car driver when he grows up."

On the other side of the coin, parents and friends may have said harsh things that tore down your self-image and made you feel insignificant or worthless.

"You'll never graduate if you keep hanging around with your friends."

"He'll never be as handsome as his father."

"You don't deserve to have a happy marriage."

This type of upbringing could convince you to get therapy as an adult to help you brush away the abusive comments and see yourself – good and bad – for who you really are.

What did your relatives and friends say about you? Did their predictions come true? If so, do you think their words subtly influenced you? Or did they notice your innate talents or weaknesses that would develop fully as an adult?

Reflect on Early Learning

When I was a young boy, I loved sports. I spent all my free time watching athletic competitions at school or on television. As I got older, I would practice my favorite sporting skills alone or with friends. Blessed with great coaches from an early age, for me, they became role models of inspiration. I noticed how they worked with each of us on the team to bring out our best qualities while teaching us how to overcome difficulties. I admired their patience in dealing with our different personalities, and I was grateful for their guidance as I learned how to play to my strengths with the rest of the team. Winning became not just about self-glorification but also about sharing the work required to support each of us on the playing field. We learned how to help one another overcome weaknesses because we shared the common goals of playing a fun game and the hope of victory.

Looking back, I can see times when leadership opportunities arose for me throughout my childhood. I was fortunate to earn the position of captain of my school's and local club's cricket teams. The practices were hard, but playing the game was a highlight of my youth. My sports interests and abilities extended to volleyball and soccer, where I also served as captain. In addition, I represented my school in gymnastic competitions, a terrific way to keep in shape between sports seasons. And for intellectual pursuits, I won our school's chess championship for three consecutive years. These achievements are mentioned not to boast but to demonstrate my intense interest in athletic and academic competition and a desire to be successful.

From age 16, I saw in myself a keen sense of competition coupled with a strong commitment to sportsmanship. I loved being part of a team and offering experience or insight to team members to help them meet or exceed the coach's expectations and support our team goals. Growing older, I started to put into practice the wisdom provided by parents, teachers, and coaches.

> One man practicing good sportsmanship is far better than 50 others preaching it. – Knute Rockne

On reflection, I recognize the seeds of leadership sown during my teenage years and the growth that followed my young adult life. I have always been thrown into leadership roles in working with youth, church activities, work duties, and family responsibilities. For more than 40 years, I have been crafting my leadership experience, sometimes without realizing it and other times while making a conscious effort.

Your life may have followed a similar pattern. Can you see the seeds of leadership sown in your childhood, teenage and young adult years? It may have been through sports, like me, or maybe you enjoyed a hobby that taught you about working with others, conflict, leadership, and life in general.

Perhaps you were involved in music or the theater or volunteered at a church, hospice center, or school. Through these early activities, you have experienced things that color your perception of certain behaviors and issues. If you helped at a food kitchen, for example, you gained insight into why people seek assistance, along with their specific needs. You might recognize patterns of behavior or certain circumstances that often require aid. Being part of a team, group or organization allows everyone to share ideas collectively and compare impressions they have gathered. It gives us skills to work productively with others and compile information about different personalities or how to work as a team. You acquire experience in analyzing suggestions and weighing opinions to access essential facts as well as different perspectives.

As you look back on your early years, think about how you benefited from the experience of mentors, coaches, or older people. Did your grandparents offer kind advice or accumulated wisdom to guide you? Did a teacher recommend participating in an extracurricular activity brought about by your interest or skills? Perhaps a coach inspired you by the way they led and modeled leadership. Did an early employer recognize abilities in you that led to a promotion or advanced assignment? Or did a good friend honestly and lovingly point out a character flaw or suggest a change?

A colleague of mine was encouraged by her fifth-grade teacher, who had noticed her writing ability, to enroll in a creative writing class to develop her skills. Although the family couldn't afford the class and she was unable to attend, her writing assignments in school continued to be admired by others. Entering her teens, she began keeping a diary and then a series of journals that she wrote periodically for many years, recording events about her dating life, marriage, children, extended family, and writing adventures. She earned college degrees in English and literature. Family members asked her for help when tackling their own writing tasks, such as a resume.

This little girl knew from an early age that she enjoyed writing, and her teacher's recommendation showed that others had faith in her abilities. As an adult, she wrote hundreds of articles, a few books, and even film screenplays by expanding her skills to do something she had always enjoyed. Today she makes a living by teaching writing classes and providing business writing workshops for professional organizations. She discovered her passion early in life and has continued to pursue it as a lifelong career.

As we look to define our character in the present, reflecting on early interests and opportunities gives us clues not only to our passions and motivations but our skills, abilities, and unique way of relating to and leading others. I encourage you to take some time to reflect on these early opportunities and what they have revealed to you about who you are today.

Talk to Family and Friends

Along with personal reflection, spend time asking people who have known you for many years what they feel your strengths are. For example, if they say you have natural oversight skills, ask how they see that in you. You supervised a younger sibling's homework by showing him how to study or taught a friend how to fish; you earned a high school award as the most helpful classmate. Your grandparents, parents, siblings, aunts and uncles, or teachers might remember special qualities you demonstrated over time – skills you didn't notice or forgot. Thinking about your abilities from others' points of view might provide clues to future leadership opportunities.

Casual chats with neighbors, teachers, or coaches may reveal qualities they became aware of as you grew up. A local grocery store owner might recall when you would step aside to let an elderly customer check out first, noting your courtesy and regard for others. The next-door neighbor might remember you as an industrious child, always helping around the house by raking the yard or carrying out rubbish. Even slight impressions like these can add to your understanding of the traits you developed as a child that contribute to who you are today. Awareness of these abilities will enable you to use them more assertively as you develop your leadership goals.

Former classmates and crushes can also fill in some gaps

by sharing memories of your early personality and behavior. You might be surprised to hear that some of your school friends thought you were naturally smart – not because of your grades but because you were the first to figure out solutions to common problems, like where to park at a busy teen hangout or forming a study group to prepare for a foreign language exam.

As you collect the various imprints you made on others' lives, images of your strengths and abilities will become more apparent. This can be a great starting place to explore the skills you were developing and see where they have led you today. Understanding your current capabilities can point you in the right direction for future leadership.

You can do this in diverse ways. Make a list of the qualities others remember about you from youth onward. Do you see any patterns? Do certain traits cluster in a specific personality type? For example, if you were motivated by sports like I was, are you in a career that relies on teamwork or physical activity, along with maneuverability tactics? Or did you grow up nurturing younger siblings or helping a single parent and are now drawn to working in a field that supports others, such as health care or education?

A graphic image like a tree cluster can help map your journey toward leadership. Try connecting the dots between what you were like as a child and how you are today. You might see that you used to enjoy putting puzzles together and conducting science lab experiments. As a result, you might be working as an architect, researcher, or digital designer. But are there secondary qualities from your past that might reveal other skills? If you raised horses, for example, do you still enjoy horseback riding or spending time in the country? Simple pleasures that bring you close to nature might be a secondary calling in your future. Or you may be able to blend it with your current career, such as taking a nursing career from an urban hospital to a rural clinic.

These correlations are not absolute. But it's interesting to think about how your childhood circumstances might have contributed to where you are today and where you would like to go in the future.

Take an Aptitude Survey

If you have collected assorted opinions about your childhood and young adult years, the next step is to analyze their degree of influence on your professional development. Some young people are so rebellious that they deliberately head in the opposite direction from where their parents and supporters would like to see them go. But even those who do can return to their strengths and re-establish their leadership potential.

Your relatives and friends from the past may have been right about your talents and abilities. But your interests might have changed, or the skills they noticed may not be useful in your current line of work. If you want to advance in your career by taking on more responsibilities and coaching others, it may be helpful to take an aptitude test.

There are many kinds of aptitude tests that gauge your interest in and knowledge of assorted topics and skills. Some measure vocabulary while others assess your math abilities. There are surveys that evaluate job preferences for working alone or with others and in accepting direction or giving it. Certain kinds of tests can determine levels of patience, tolerance, diligence, and other qualities. Some employers will conduct aptitude tests to decide how to develop employees to be multiskilled or to acquire needed job skills.

You can also take an aptitude test on your own like one of the following:

aptitude-test.com by Seliant. This free online aptitude test lasts about 12 minutes. Scores are organized into categories that include numerical reasoning and abstract thinking. You can learn about the way you approach problems and interpret information.

thebalancecareers.com. This service offers aptitude tests to help you learn more about your personal and professional interests.

There are many other aptitude tests. Some surveys take just a few minutes, and your responses are recorded and summarized for immediate review. An assessment of your answers may be provided, along with a grid or key to help you understand the results. You might not agree with everything in the report, but it is a starting place to analyze your professional interests and inclinations objectively. You can also take two or more aptitude tests and compare the results.

Keep a Journal

Start writing about your career goals in a handwritten or digital journal. Write about the daily activities in your job and how these contribute or not to job satisfaction and career fulfillment. In an article titled "6 Ways Keeping a Journal Can Help Your Career," author Jenna (Britton) Arak explains that writing about your job helps you jot down promising ideas, recall lessons learned, and record advice from leaders and mentors. You can vent confidentially, store compliments, and plan.[1]

Journals are an excellent way of capturing and reflecting on key moments in your professional life. In fact, studies have shown journaling can reduce stress and improve health for conditions like back problems. Reducing tension can help you think more creatively and work more productively.

Suggestions for keeping a personal journal:

1. Keep your journal private, so you can write honestly about your observations.

2. Designate a certain time each day, for example, after getting up or before bed. While the time may fluctuate, sticking to the approximate same time each day will help form a habit.

3. Try to write three to five days per week for a few minutes each time.

4. Focus on your job. Record positive and negative experiences about what went well and what could have been better. You can theorize how to manage the situation more effectively in the future.

5. Include specific details, like the dates and times when key events occurred. This information will help maintain an objective and accurate record rather than subjective and vague impressions.

Occasionally, review your journal for information about the leadership you have observed in others, as well as your own tendencies to lead. What did your supervisor do that was truly admirable or inspiring? What type of mistake happened that you would not want to repeat?

Every few months, reread what you've written. Have you adjusted your work based on recorded events or impressions? Did you identify new or improved strengths or find hidden weaknesses? Your journal can become a journey of self-discovery as you thoughtfully assess workplace conditions that impact the development of your leadership potential for negotiating differences and mitigating conflict. You can also recognize successful actions on which to build.

Many professionals keep a journal or daily log of workplace highs and lows. They refer to this record informally and privately or share it with a supervisor at the annual performance review. Keeping relevant job information on hand enables you to track your progress, along with any setbacks to improve your workplace performance.

Analyze Your Weaknesses

Just as you talked to relatives and friends about your strengths, ask about the weaknesses they perceived. They might reveal the trivial lies you used to tell, like children sometimes do. Or they may recall your father making you clean a friend's yard after a littering incident with schoolmates. Maybe you will recall, as one of my friends recently did, a theft incident. My friend, at age six, stole a strawberry at the grocery store and tucked it into the pocket of her yellow shirt. At the checkout counter, unnoticed by her father, who had accompanied her and was paying for groceries, she was horrified to discover the strawberry was liquifying from the heat and staining her shirt's chest pocket bright red. She was so scared of being caught that she never stole again!

Rather than these types of instances, however, when we analyze our weaknesses, it is more to reflect on the desirable career qualities that you may lack or have only in a small quantity. For example, you might be weak at numerical calculations or be too shy to converse easily with strangers in public. Knowing your weaknesses will help you either avoid situations where they might be exposed or enable you to work on getting stronger in those areas. If you are shy or reserved, you might not be comfortable in a customer service position, but you might feel good about writing customer service policies without much direct interaction with the public.

You will have your own ideas about your workplace strengths and weaknesses. But other people's perceptions may differ. For example, you might feel you are a great motivator because you set the bar high and expect everyone else to do the same. But in certain jobs, employees may need coaching or support to reach that level of performance. They might require discipline, motivation, or recognition. You might have to learn to be flexible. We often believe ourselves to be the best judge of our character, but sometimes those around us can see things we miss.

Address Your Weaknesses

After learning what those closest to you believe to be your weaknesses, make a list, and see if you agree. Cross out the ones you are sure you have dealt with or outgrown. Put a checkmark next to those on which you want to work. Review your annual job performance evaluations to see if you are addressing areas of mediocrity or weakness.

Be open to making improvements. If you have been carelessly late to work several times in the past year, make changes to arrive on time. If you are struggling to learn a new procedure at your job, ask a coworker to help after work or do some online research at home. If your annual job performance review indicates that you are doing an average amount of work, look for ways to boost your performance to a higher level. If you are tempted to take shortcuts at your job, resolve to stop. If you get easily angered by a coworker's slack performance, learn to direct your frustration more effectively than lashing out or complaining to others.

A responsible manager or resolute leader sets the example for those under their purview. Obviously, you want to set a positive example. Occasional mistakes will occur, but they should be acknowledged and addressed in a fair and honest manner. Leaders who don't honestly appraise or accept criticism for themselves cannot be trusted to evaluate other employees objectively.

Being called on the carpet is not just a disciplinary action. It's also an opportunity to make things right. Many successful leaders will tell you that the mistakes they made are just as valuable in their professional development as the strengths they cultivated.

Is there anything on which you can improve? Olga Rogacka's article, "12 Stories from Leaders: Their Mistakes and Lessons Learned," advises that leadership begins with getting to know yourself, including your strengths and weaknesses. She suggests you must let yourself make mistakes that teach valuable lessons. Her article includes 12 common mistakes from established managers and leaders who share firsthand experiences:

1. Blaming others for mistakes
2. Allowing your perfectionism to influence the team
3. Micromanaging
4. Making important decisions based on emotions
5. Jumping to conclusions without double-checking with an employee
6. Expecting everyone to do the job the same way you do
7. Delegating tasks the wrong way
8. Correcting employees' mistakes
9. Talking and directing over listening and guiding

10. Pushing too hard
11. Relying too much on a resume
12. Forgetting about work-life balance.[2]

Do any of these sound familiar? Although managers shared their stories in this article, any employee can make similar errors when working with others, leading a team, or even when working independently. Of course, there are additional mistakes that we can make on the job, but these give you a broad idea of weaknesses that managers recognize in themselves and take steps to correct.

Have you ever been accused of errors like these? What did you do about it?

The natural human response to weaknesses attributed to us is often self-defense. We rationalize, make excuses, claim forgetfulness, and pass the blame, along with other behaviors that are not credible, admirable, or ethical. When someone points the finger at you and reveals a weakness in your job performance, consider responding as follows:

- Listen carefully and take notes
- Summarize or repeat the claim to ensure you've understood correctly
- Ask for supporting details, examples, or evidence if warranted
- Request time, if needed, to review your records or check the facts
- Admit the weakness or mistake honestly and humbly
- Apologize
- Offer to make amends to everyone involved
- Deal with that weakness to ensure it doesn't keep happening.

An interesting observation about celebrities embroiled in scandals is that the public is often willing to forgive them – if they acknowledge a mistake and apologize. Those who try to cover their tracks and deny responsibility often lose whatever respect might be left following their mistake.

In the workplace, credibility and responsibility are critical for leadership success.

- Attend all scheduled meetings, even when coworkers are skipping them.
- Arrive on time and don't leave early.
- Don't exploit your lunch break unless you have an appointment.
- Show kindness and respect to all.
- If you have a grievance with someone, discuss it privately and politely.
- Give someone a hand if they need it without compromising your own workload.
- Offer suggestions for improvement without sounding critical or condescending.
- Be willing to let other employees have the premier parking spot or vacation dates.
- Work overtime if requested when it works with your other responsibilities.
- Treat others the way you want to be treated, especially from a managerial role.

Other easy things you can do: Smile and be friendly. Don't take your personal troubles to work. Avoid talkative peers who keep you from doing your job. Do everything you are asked to do without complaining and do it to the best of your ability.

You will be noticed, and you might be offered a pay raise or a promotion.

Next Steps

By now, you should be thinking about the career position you have, or hope to have soon, and your leadership potential within the organization. Using the suggested activities in this chapter, you may have a more specific idea of the qualities you have or will need to assume a managerial role in the company. Here is a summary of your journey so far:

- Take aptitude tests to help you find the job you want
- Write in a journal for work-based experiences to record thoughts and feelings
- Review performance reports that indicate your strengths and weaknesses
- Practice ways of overcoming weaknesses and building strengths.

Roberta Matuson's LinkedIn article, "Evergreen Leadership Lessons from the Ever Given Fiasco," raises a valid point about the importance of informed leaders:

Be clear on where you're headed and have your charts on hand. Leaders have a general sense of where the company is headed, but sometimes they aren't privy to the plan that plots out how the organization will get safely to its stated destination.[3]

As you prepare for a leadership role, ensure you have all the relevant information needed to make clear decisions about the job you want, the type of company you would like to work for, and the prospect of leadership in your future. You can't jump from Level H to Level A without first working through the maze of education, experience, training, and evaluation.

Below is a leadership assessment and goals survey. Work through the items as best you can, even if some do not seem to fit your current circumstances. You may want to confidentially discuss the survey with a family member or colleague for their feedback, or you may prefer to keep it private. Either way, the survey elicits things to consider as you contemplate your career path and leadership options.

Leadership Assessment and Goals Survey

1. I am currently employed in my chosen career field.
   ☐ Yes   ☐ No

2. I am reasonably sure of being employed in my chosen career within 6 to 12 months.
   ☐ Yes   ☐ No

3. I do not have a preferred career or a secure career path currently.
   ☐ Yes   ☐ No

4. I am prepared (education, certifications, experience) for a job in my chosen field but cannot apply now.
   ☐ Yes   ☐ No

5. I am currently acquiring education, certifications, experience, and training to get a career position.
   ☐ Yes   ☐ No

6. I have held leadership roles at work in the past for six months or longer.
   ☐ Yes   ☐ No

Define Your Character

7. I have held a leadership role for up to six months.
   ☐ Yes ☐ No

8. I have taken specific leadership training at work.
   ☐ Yes ☐ No

9. I have worked at several jobs but have not yet established a career.
   ☐ Yes ☐ No

10. I consider myself a compliant employee and respectful of authority.
    ☐ Yes ☐ No

11. I believe other employees (current or in the future) would follow my leadership.
    ☐ Yes ☐ No

12. Leaders should rule with an iron fist to ensure employee compliance.
    ☐ Yes ☐ No

13. Employee rights and individual needs should be considered by leaders in assigning jobs.
    ☐ Yes ☐ No

14. I enjoy helping people at work to meet their goals or learn new skills.
    ☐ Yes ☐ No

15. I prefer working independently away from the distractions of coworkers.
    ☐ Yes ☐ No

16. I have been told by other leaders that I have leadership qualities or potential.
    ☐ Yes ☐ No

17. I might have difficulty with certain leadership duties, like finances or firing people.
    ☐ Yes ☐ No

18. I generally get along with most people.
    ☐ Yes ☐ No

19. Although not yet a leader, I don't mind learning new things that can help me become a better employee.
    ☐ Yes ☐ No

20. My main leadership goals are to support or improve productivity and employee wellbeing.
    ☐ Yes ☐ No

Results:

If you answered "Yes" to questions 1, 4, 5, 8, 13, 15, 16 and 20 you seem to be on track to become a leader in your chosen career field.

If you answered "Yes" to questions 2, 3, 6, 7, 9, 10, 11, 12, 14, 17, 18 and 19 you may want to further develop your career interests before deciding whether to pursue a leadership role.

Note: This survey does not equate to or replace a certified aptitude test like those described earlier in the chapter.

Summary

The suggestions in this chapter are made without knowing you personally. You may prefer to consider other ways of establishing a career and becoming a leader. There are many paths to success, and you should explore all that may be useful.

In the next chapter, we will look at ways to get the job you want and make the most of your workplace experience. The same approach will be used to help you think about the type of leadership role you feel suited for.

Keep in mind that finding the right role takes time. If you are committed to the task, you should soon begin to find answers to your leadership questions.

Chapter 2

Pursue Your Passion

Chapter 1 discussed tools to recognize your leadership interests and potential characteristics. You are beginning to learn how to pursue your passions to find a meaningful and lucrative job where you can use your talents and skills. You can also start to help others develop their workplace strengths. A good leader is not just someone who tells people what to do but supports employees by explaining and demonstrating how to reach goals and build excellent work habits and skills.

You might have always known that you prefer working outdoors rather than sitting at a desk in a stuffy office. But how do you know for which outdoor occupation you are best suited? You might decide to become a forest ranger, a geothermal engineer, or a landscaper. Each of those careers offer – and sometimes require – leadership roles. But you don't want to get stuck in the wrong position, leading to a dead end for your career goals.

Think back to your teen years. Was there a school subject or extracurricular activity you loved? Were you able to pursue your heartfelt interests? Did your parents support you or try to steer you in another direction? You wanted to become a football star while they bought you a flute for high school band. Did family members support you in your selected career path?

If you have followed your dream or reclaimed it along the way, you might be ready to become an expert. Many paths lead to proficiency, though it will take time. You might already have several years of experience doing what you love. The more knowledgeable you are at doing what you enjoy, the greater your chance of success, and you will develop natural leadership tendencies at the same time because you are emotionally invested.

During my growing up years, from age ten or so, I used to do the newspaper run in my district and surrounding areas, selling and distributing the *Daily News* and the *Sunday Tribune*. From that job, I learned how to budget my time between school, home chores, and the paper deliveries. My stepmom worked for a family as their maid, and they let her bring home flowers from their garden, along with ferns and old newspapers. We arranged attractive bundles, and I would sell these in the neighborhood to earn a little extra income. From that work, I learned to be thrifty and recycle things that could be reused in profitable ways.

For a time, I also worked in a market, where I gained experience organizing the produce and assisting customers. Later I had a position as a bus conductor, collecting fares for the driver. This role taught me to be pleasant and dependable with the public. At one point, I helped my neighbors when they extended their home by chipping in with errands or small jobs that were interesting, such as hammering boards or installing tiles. For a time, I got involved in assisting some motor mechanics, from whom I learned about motor technology.

Although minor, all these experiences added to my growing list of skills, as well as how to get along with the public. I took those jobs because of challenging economic times. But on reflection, these tasks acquainted me with demanding work and prepared me to train others from a leadership perspective that I've continued to learn along the way.

No job experience goes to waste. Nor does working with people in any capacity, whether in a paid position or as a volunteer. Think about the work you've done and the skills you've learned throughout your life. How have they prepared you for future leadership?

Become an Expert

Once you have decided on the passion you want to pursue, you will need to develop the expertise to excel in it. Expertise evolves in many ways. You may know people who became experts through education, job experience, or professional training. There are proven methods that can help you master the role in which you want to excel. Some are based on your preferred approach to becoming an expert.

For example, if you are employed full-time and have a family, you might want to spend time reading extensively in your area of interest at your convenience. If you are a college student or a young professional, you could get a position as an intern or volunteer for firsthand experience in the type of organization where you would one day like to work full-time.

Since you will need to develop a certain level of expertise to prepare for a managerial or leadership role, let's look at some ways you can establish a specialty niche in your job field.

Write a Leadership Development Plan

As you can to see, pursuing your career interests may involve significant writing. But writing is an excellent learning tool. The act of using a pen or typing on the keyboard stimulates neurons in the brain to make meaning from your thoughts and feelings to create a guiding path that leads to a plan. Since everyone can decide how to become an expert, it is important to develop a plan that will correlate with your professional interests, aptitude, availability, and current job to help you build relevant experience. Here's an example of a development plan for a full-time outdoor career:

Become a Landscape Company Owner with 10–15 Employees:
- Take landscaping or horticulture classes
- Recruit a seasoned landscaper as a mentor
- Read books and watch how-to videos
- Register for local landscaping workshops
- Get a landscaper assistant job
- Join landscaping organizations.

You can flesh out a plan in more detail as you get started. When you have time, research the names of landscapers to contact for part-time work as well as the vocational school or college where you can take landscaping or horticulture classes and browse the library or bookstores for books or videos. More action steps to put your plan in motion might include identifying business organizations to join and participating in area landscaping or gardening clubs. You can decide which steps to follow.

In your goal to become a leader, writing a development plan will map out basic steps to take you in the right direction. Start by exploring practical ways of matching your aptitude to a talent or skill, then write a career plan that will help you learn everything you need to know. Continue to refine your skills as you advance in that field.

Research leadership opportunities within your desired

job field to determine the type of position you want to obtain. Recent college graduates can work with the campus job placement service to learn more about the job they want. A placement advisor can explain common job duties, required training, and the average starting salary. Your plan to develop job expertise could include less conventional approaches. You may want to participate in local trade shows or observe DIY store demonstrations. You can surf the Web to find expert blogs and vlogs. If you have friends or neighbors in the business, casually interview them about their work to learn more from a practical perspective.

When it is impractical for you to get a part-time job in your field of interest, volunteer a couple of days each month to get familiar with the work and help a local company at the same time. Even unloading bricks or mixing concrete can be a learning experience. As an added incentive, you will get to know people in the business who may offer future employment or guidance.

Be creative in developing ways to expand your knowledge of the job you want. Typically, you will need to consider education, qualified guidance (i.e., a mentor or advisor), active learning on the job, and professional involvement as conventional steps towards your career development.

Some career experts recommend dressing and behaving like someone who holds the position you would like to have. This will prepare you for the role and influence others to visualize you in that position.

Find a Focus

The next step of your personalized leadership training will be to choose a niche in your occupation, if possible. This doesn't mean that you can't do various kinds of work. It just means you can build your expertise in a specific area. In doing so, you are becoming a leader who will be ready to teach and guide others who follow a similar path.

In our landscaping example, you might choose to excel in hardscapes. That type of landscaping involves working with structural substances like concrete, stone, and wood to build walls or design walkways for residential or commercial properties. By developing an expertise, you are advancing your brand and promoting your business further. As your experience and knowledge increase, you can establish your role or company publicly. Emphasize your skills in marketing campaigns and a social media presence. As public interest grows, you may decide to work on another specialization as you continue to build your customer base and position yourself as a multiskilled expert. Follow your interests to do the work you love, and you will naturally develop a leadership attitude when developing your career and in working with others to share what you have learned.

In choosing a focus for your career plan, take the following steps:

1. **Develop a vision.** Consider the niche in which you would enjoy specializing. Think about where you would like to spend much of your time on the job. Is this an area where you can become a leader to train and guide employees, or is it an independent contractor role? How might your leadership become an asset to the industry and benefit customers?

2. **Write a business plan.** Create an outline for pursuing your occupation and establishing a specialty niche. It may come naturally over time or be something you have recently learned to love. To become effectively qualified,

plan your objectives and short-term as well as long-term goals as a series of doable steps, which will make the journey less demanding.

3. **Find learning resources.** There are many ways to learn all you can about the role you want to master in your occupation. Scout the Internet for articles, videos, and demonstrations. Join business groups and get acquainted with members in your industry. Visit local companies or sites where you can observe your specialty in practice.

4. **Talk about it.** Meet with others in the field to discuss how they got started. Share your goal with those you trust. They may offer practical tips or leads. Contact local businesses to see if they can refer you to specialists or additional resources that you haven't yet discovered.

5. **Take small steps.** Be diligent and patient. It takes time to learn how to do a new job well. It will take even more time to become a recognized leader in your field to influence employees and attract customers. Recognize each milestone that you reach. Check your progress routinely to find out what is working versus what needs to be changed for better results.

While you are eager to make fast progress and see positive results, enjoy the journey instead of rushing to your destination. You might find another interesting or lucrative specialty along the way or discover new and better ways of reaching your goals.

As you begin your quest, periodically evaluate your progress:

- **Make sure you are comfortable in your selected niche.** Even if the specialty you are eyeing is popular, are you really interested in doing the work? For example, pest control often features specializations for removing certain pests like bats or rodents. But if that does not interest you, there's no point in getting involved just to increase your marketability unless income is a primary goal or need.

- **Ensure you have the skills or aptitude to become an expert.** Some professional niches may seem like dazzling prospects. You might like the idea of earning a business degree and becoming a personal assistant for a CEO while working your way to a managerial position. But if you don't want to spend your workday arranging meetings, making presentations, or providing technological support, this might not be a satisfying niche for you. Consider a range of options when making your choice.

- **Take stock of resources.** As you develop your business and establish a specialty niche, look for ways to enhance your skills with the help of local resources. These might include mentors, local contractors, business groups, civic organizations, and government grants or guidelines. You should also devote time each week to researching your niche area to learn all you can. If you use social media, explore sites like LinkedIn or Twitter for reliable sources of information.

- **Find out if there is a market for your specialty.** Survey your target market to see which services customers want before choosing a specialty area. A freelance writer who provides Web content and business articles might want to develop a specialty as a company history writer, for example. But if there is a small demand for this service, it might not be a useful or lucrative niche. Socialize to build business relationships. Schedule lunch with an expert you admire. It doesn't have to be someone in your vocational field. It could be a successful person who has built a career that led to leadership roles in ways that you would like to emulate.

An organic route to preparing for leadership is budget-friendly without a major investment of time or money. It can also be personally and professionally fulfilling as you utilize tools and strategies to build your leadership potential.

Share What You Know

You can begin sharing the knowledge you've accumulated before you become a fully-fledged success. There's room for more than one person at a time on the ladder to success. According to Jim Rohn of *Success* magazine, remarkable things can happen to move your career forward while helping other people:

> The key to make your life really unique and worthwhile is to share what you know, because sharing has a certain unique magic of its own.
>
> If you share an idea with ten different people, they get to hear it once and you get to hear it ten times – getting you even better prepared for the future. Share ideas with your family, with the people around you, with other employees, with your colleagues.
>
> If you share with someone else, they could be trans-

formed. You may have dropped in at the right time – this may be their moment, the moment the door will open and there's opportunity they never saw before...

But here's what else is exciting: The person who speaks could be transformed, too. Because guess what, we're all looking for transformation for our new life – the new life tomorrow, this month, this year, next year.[4]

Many Instagram influencers are young, some in their teens. But they have developed exceptional skills or knowledge, ranging from fashion to finances, which global viewers are keen to learn. While developing their brand of expertise, they earn income from social media outlets by sharing what they know with an interested public.

As you build your skills towards a leadership role, you can establish yourself as an expert by helping others in roles like teaching, tutoring, mentoring, demonstrating, or training. You can teach others the skills you have mastered while continuing your journey. You also will become a model of success that will enhance your leadership potential.

There are many ways to go public with your expertise and area of specialization. Your marketing choices will depend on the formats you prefer and the costs involved. Here are some of the most effective ways to establish your niche as a leader-in-training.

Internet

- **Website.** If you are employed, your company might have a webpage for you or your department. Make sure it's updated with your current credentials. If permitted, you might want to add a favorite quote or a professional photo. The company website will be your ladder, so to

Pursue Your Passion

speak, that will lead to the heights of your career, where you become an authorized or de facto company leader. This is where those who want to know more about you will begin their research.

- **Digital Newsletter.** If your company publishes an in-house or public newsletter, it may request employee submissions. Offer occasional articles about your unit's current initiatives or recent achievements – not to boast but to keep everyone aware of your progress. Whenever your name and photo appear in print, you will gain respect from those who become acquainted with you and what you do.

    As an expert-in-training, you could also submit opinion pieces or how-to articles to local business newsletters to keep your subscribers up to date with your knowledge and skills. You can include recent company successes to build readers' awareness and faith in your product and expertise.

    An e-mail newsletter is a fantastic way to inform subscribers about your evolving specialty. As you gain recognition and earn readers' trust and respect, you will be seen as an expert who is earning awareness as a leader in the field.

- **Video Conferencing.** When you are responsible for arranging Zoom calls or other video conferences, give them your best effort. Be prepared by sending an agenda in advance to the participants. Cultivate a professional and accessible image through the way you dress and the attitude you project. You might want to include PowerPoint slides or other media to support the main points of your topic. Be sure to give everyone a chance to speak and show respect for their comments, even when you disagree. A video conference is like an interview for a leadership position. People will be watching to see how you manage the agenda issues, how informative and organized you are, and how you interact with others. These observations create an impression that will affect participants' opinions of your ability to organize and lead a meeting that will garner results.

Video lets you shine in the role of guide that puts you in the driver's seat. That is what leaders do, so you are giving a preview performance of your leadership abilities.

- **E-Commerce.** When participating in e-commerce, your colleagues and potential customers will begin to recognize your face over time. Create a positive impression with an upbeat message that offers a solution to a real or potential problem. Showing that you have the answers they need will encourage them to do business with you as someone knowledgeable and dependable.

  Consider in general terms the type of leader you would like to be and how you want others to see you. Package your profile around your products in online marketing strategies by depicting yourself through appearance, manner, and personality type as the leader you are becoming.

- **Social Media.** If you already have social media accounts on Facebook or LinkedIn, you might want to include Instagram and Twitter to build a following by sharing your expertise with a broad range of followers. You've probably watched videos on practical tasks like how to do an oil change for your car or removing wallpaper before painting a room. You don't have to come across as a celebrity, but it does help to offer valuable tips, suggestions, and fresh information to people who subscribe to your site. The more help you can responsibly provide, the likelier your social media site will attract more followers.

Happy followers will tell others about you. Word of mouth is one of the best and easiest ways to promote awareness of your brand to consumers or the public at large.

In addition to posting your own content, comment on the sites of professionals you admire. Their followers may admire your posts and look for your site as well.

- **Text Message Marketing.** Although marketing text messages are annoying to some people, you might be able to craft a brief message that will resonate with certain readers. It might be a motivational quote or a helpful reminder to keep up with six-month dental cleanings. Find a way to send useful messages, quotes, or insights with a link to your social media accounts to attract new followers. Offer an "unsubscribe" or "do not text me" option.

  Avoid using emojis, as they can be confusing. Keep your message simple and straightforward.

- **Book Reviews.** If you like to read, you might enjoy posting online reviews of your favorite business books. Fans of those authors who find your reviews insightful may gravitate to your website or social media accounts, especially if you post information on recent best sellers in the same genre. As you become known for thoughtful book evaluations, readers will look for your posts on publications they find interesting to see what you have to say. In that way, you will attain a leading role by becoming a noteworthy literary critic in publications related to your profession.

A quality book review needs to be professionally written. Edit and proofread your posts before posting them. You can also hire a writing coach or editor to polish your writing before it is published. Skillful writing makes a powerful impression on readers. Avoid biased language and offer thoughtful assessments of the author's ideas and style.

- **Blog or Vlog.** Starting a blog or a vlog (video blog) about your industry, sector, or job can help you build an online presence as an influencer or expert. You probably subscribe to blogs and vlogs of experts you trust, and you might leave a supportive comment when they address a topic of mutual interest.

  If a company employs you, you might have to clear online promotions with your supervisor first. Some employers require complete disclosure of employees' activities that may reflect directly or indirectly on the company's image. Other companies don't mind social media interactions if you maintain a professional image and don't compete with your employer's interests.

  When you are self-employed, you can publish a blog or vlog about your business. Establish an online presence that will attract viewers by posting two or three times weekly and using compelling headlines or titles. Your online persona should be professional enough to convince readers of the validity of your views. Some vloggers video-record themselves or post images of their products.

- **Interviews.** As you establish your brand through an online presence and professional contacts, you might be approached for an interview by local radio or television talk shows that feature area experts. Sometimes an online organization will request an interview as well, as recently happened to a colleague who resides in the United States but was interviewed for a United Kingdom publication. If you are not directly asked, you can offer local media and online entities an interview about recent innovations or company plans as well as professional developments.

    For example, if you are a graphic designer who has created a new digital, interactive greeting card, you may want to explain how it works in a public interview. This would reflect well on your employer or your business, along with your designer skills. Of course, you can't reveal proprietary secrets. But you can explain the distinctions of the new greeting card design that add value to the industry.

Publications

- **Newspaper Articles.** Although print media is not as widespread as it used to be, many communities still publish a print version of the news – often in conjunction with the digital edition. You might be able to contribute a local interest piece on your company's development of a new product that will interest the public. You will need the company's permission, of course. If given, your article will make you the face of the organization, at least for this bit of news, and help define your public image.

    A letter to the editor of a newspaper or magazine as an employee or individual can add to your reputation when you write about a topic related to your area of specialization.

For example, Elena is a metro park ranger who has led guided tours through the metro parklands for 15 years. One of her specialties is coniferous trees. As an expert, she works with horticulturalists and landscapers in recommending the best soil types and watering techniques to promote healthy growth of these trees, with blue spruce as one of her specialties. She gives interviews, authors articles, and makes presentations to community groups like schools and garden clubs. She is acknowledged as a leader in the local park industry, although she does not hold that specific title. Elena is often contacted for help with local tree growth and land management projects.

- **Magazine Articles.** A magazine article is usually longer and more in-depth than a newspaper article. Depending on the publication, it might be based on research and cite experts or include a profile of an industry leader. Magazines featuring articles about your specialty area typically should appeal to a broad audience of readers, which can help promote your ideas as someone with vision. Publishing with respected magazines and journals adds credentials to your resume. Your work could remain in print for years and be archived indefinitely.

    If you cite reputable sources and your article is accepted in a respected publication, your professional image will be even more polished as an expert on that topic.

- **Trade Publications.** Magazines and journals related to a specific industry, like air travel or military service, often seek contributed articles by experts or former personnel. So if you work in the rubber industry and hope to specialize as a consultant on aircraft flotation devices, you may be able to submit articles related to the safe use of these devices to an aviation magazine.

- **Training Seminar or Course.** Employees or entrepreneurs who work with specific programs can often package their experience into a training seminar or course format. Ben, who works in the food service industry, has developed a dirty dish collection tray that makes loading items into the dishwasher faster and easier. He gives talks and demonstrations to local restaurants and has developed a five-minute online video. Ben is now working on another strategy for dishwasher design that he hopes to patent. With these achievements growing in popularity, he is becoming known as an industry innovator and is invited to show his wares at national and international trade shows.

- **E-Book.** Self-publishing an e-book about your professional work is another way to build a leadership platform. E-books are short and simple. They outline a process or describe a strategy for achieving a specific goal. Examples might be something like *8 Ways to Reduce Waste at Work* or *12 Must-Have Home Office Time Savers*.
  Some people who want to build an impressive resume publish e-books. If you can offer readers something they might not have but truly want, your e-book could help you climb another step or two on your ladder to success.

- **Self-Published Print Book.** On a larger publishing scale, to strengthen your specialty platform, you could publish a regular book in electronic or print format – or both. Several self-publishing companies offer free or low-cost publication of your book, with royalties split between the publisher and the author. Many authors have established themselves as experts by self-publishing a book. Sometimes a traditional press will buy the rights to the book and publish it in the conventional way, which results in wider exposure and increased revenue.

Compare self-publishing programs to see their fees and how they can help. Authoring a book underscores your expert status and may generate speaking invitations and interviews. Public talks and presentations underscore your leadership role in the subject area of your book.

- **Professional Presentations.** Depending on your line of work, you may be asked to give a presentation for the company or at one of its branches. Adding this skill to your resume will contribute to your expert identity. You may subsequently be invited to present a paper or participate in a roundtable discussion at a regional, national, or international conference. The more presentations you give, with additional tweaking of your topic in response to audience questions, the more seasoned you will become as an expert in that topic.

  A mid-level manager, Mark, found he had a knack for mitigating coworkers' disputes while participating in team projects. With further research, he developed a specialty in initiative-taking team dynamics and was invited to share his strategies at local business events. Within a couple of years, he was invited to make presentations to larger audiences at conferences and online venues.

Share your expertise with audiences who want to hear about it. As they become familiar with your brand and your image, they will see you as an expert. In turn, this can contribute to your preparation for a leadership role.

- **Community Involvement.** In addition to workplace and industry contributions, you can also build your credentials in the community. This might be a physical community in your hometown or an online community with members from anywhere in the world. In participating or hosting key events, you will have the opportunity to exchange ideas with others. Your acquired knowledge will shine through. Your willingness to take the lead in business or local issues can brand you a leader.

There are many ways to become the leader you want to be. But the key point is that these methods are affordable, easy, and convenient. With or without an advanced university degree, you can use strategies like these to excel at what you do. Get involved by giving expert talks, motivating colleagues, and contributing your talents to the local community.

Through study, work, exploration, and interactions, you can reach the top of the ladder as a leader who informs and inspires others – naturally and organically.

Chapter 3

Assess Your Potential to Lead

Wherever you are presently on your career journey, there are still things to learn. You might feel that you have "arrived" professionally after earning a college degree or getting the job of your dreams. But prospective leaders continue to absorb the latest information and translate life experiences into knowledge that can help them become even more effective. They share information with others on a similar path who can benefit, including the employees they oversee at work and professional colleagues in workgroups or project teams.

Lifelong learning is a common goal amongst successful leaders. Today's managers, supervisors, and administrators continually tap into the constant flow of information online and through instant and constant communication. They connect with others to learn new ways of thinking and doing things. Reading plays a huge role in leadership growth, as suggested by this anonymous quote: "If you want to be a leader, you have to be a reader."

Last year I shared the following on a social media post. One of the things I was impressed with while visiting South Korea in 2013 was the massive number of bookstores and libraries open to the public. It dawned on me that the strength of a nation is investing in its people by teaching and emphasizing the importance of reading and writing. I want to encourage you to keep reading, writing, and dispensing words of life that build, encourage, strengthen, and bring hope. Lack of communication and negligence between supervisors and coworkers is one of the greatest deficiencies and problems of the 21st-century workplace.

Let me explain with a historical example. Karl Marx devoted his life to writing about the demise of capitalism and the evolution of communism. Along with Friedrich Engels, he wrote one the most well-known political treatises in history, the *Communist Manifesto*. As evidence of his keen understanding of the great power of words, Marx was credited with saying, "Give me 26 lead soldiers, and I will conquer the world."

Who were the 26 lead soldiers Marx referred to? They are the 26 letters of the alphabet on a printing press! Language is power, or as the maxim indicates, "The pen is mightier than the sword."

All words have power and meaning.

The famous book of Proverbs in the Bible informs us that "Life and death are in the power of the tongue, and those who love it will eat its fruit" (18:21).[5]

The question is not if words have power. The question is this: What power am I releasing with my words?

The greatest untapped source of healing is pleasant words. If you have sent forth words that hurt, take them back with an apology and replace them with words that heal. You may not consider yourself a physician, but you should if you are dispensing words of life.

In the business world and beyond, as a new employee or seasoned leader, learn to speak, write, publish, and print words of life for your generation and the generations to come. How can you do this on the job? Maintain an upbeat tone in your e-mails. If you must deliver unwelcome news, use the sandwich approach by starting with a positive or neutral statement before revealing the bad news, then closing the message with a positive or hopeful look to the future.

For example, if you must write an incident report about an employee who lost her temper with a coworker, try to include an encouraging statement that indicates the employee's reason for lashing out was heard, and she was advised to address similar situations more professionally by having discussions with the coworker involved or with a supervisor. "Mary's long and successful history with the company suggests she will be able to make this adjustment expertly in a timely manner."

All of us must keep up with the evolving times. While you may not agree with workplace changes, you should respond as needed to their impact. Effective leaders learn how to learn, which involves more than just thinking about how to do things. In her article in *Forbes*, Kay Peterson explains the nature of learning by leaders:

> Most people believe that learning is a process of thinking, but that's only one step in the larger process of learning from experience. You also have to involve your feelings, perceptions, and actions.[6]

Peterson believes there are different learning styles, and some people have more than one:

> As a leader, you can raise your self-awareness every day by zooming out to notice how you use this learning process. Are you guided by your gut-level feelings of experiencing and sometimes overwhelmed by them? Or are you logical, even detached, from using thinking?

Do you jump into acting to get things done on time, often before taking time to know that you are moving in the right direction? Or does your penchant for perfection prompt you to linger in reflecting, sometimes missing opportunities?[7]

When you know your best learning approach, you can process information more effectively. Leaders learn so they can teach and inspire others. When they stop learning, their influence grows stale.

Although there are many ways to actively learn things each day, there are successful methods that help busy people continue to build knowledge. When processed, applied, and vetted, knowledge turns into wisdom, one of the most valuable commodities a leader will need. When you stop learning, your brain can begin dying.

Reading

An article that appeared on *Inc.com*, titled "Reading Habits of the Most Successful Leaders That Can Change Your Life Too," reveals surprising facts about the busiest and most successful leaders on the planet: Warren Buffett reads 500 pages per day – and when he was starting out, he read 600 to 1,000 pages per day. Here's what he says:

> That's how knowledge works. It builds up, like compound interest. All of you can do it, but I guarantee that not many of you will do it.

Another mogul, Bill Gates, reads 50 books per year.

Inspirational speaker Tony Robbins grew up in a home dominated by alcoholism and dysfunction. Reading books became a lifeline to which he attributes his leadership success. After taking a speed-reading course, he completed 700 books in seven years.[8]

Joseph Addison, a 17th-century author, wrote, "Reading is to the mind what exercise is to the body." We should all read on a regular basis to improve our minds.

Books, business articles, and professional blogs provide limitless ideas and perspectives. A huge amount of information is widely available at no cost through public libraries and online sources. For modest sums, you can invest in a subscription to a career-related publication or buy relevant books online or at a bookshop.

Leaders or leaders-in-training benefit in many ways from reading regularly:

- **Reading broadens your perspective on life.** Books introduce you to other views and situations. Your ability to understand and evaluate begins to widen.

- **Reading connects you to people, not just imaginary characters in a novel, but also real individuals who share your tastes and experiences.** It helps to read opposing opinions as well. There may be times when, as a leader, you will face a scenario that recalls a book you've read. The reading experience can help prepare you for that real-life experience. That happens to me frequently.

- **Reading exercises your analytical skills.** As you observe people and events in a specific framework, you learn how those situations played out. These stories add to your repertoire of assessment tools used in daily life and on the job.

Because it is easy to forget much of what we read, you may want to create a reading log for handy reference. When reviewed, the log reminds you of key points you don't want to forget. Here's an example of a reading log that you can keep on your computer and update whenever you read another article, book, or publication that contributes to your knowledge base.

Date Read	Title	Author	Topic/Theme	Key Points
May 2021	*What It Takes: Lessons in the Pursuit of Excellence*	Stephen A. Schwarzman, Chairman, CEO, and Co-Founder of Blackstone	His personal life experiences about building, transforming, and leading thriving organizations	- Go big - Find opportunities - Interconnect - Don't dodge crisis - Ask for help - Be the best

The more you read works of substance, the more well-rounded your intellect will become. That is a useful tool for any leader.

Ed Fernyhough's article, "How Reading Changes Your Brain," offers interesting facts about how reading affects the brain by referencing research studies:

> In 2009, Timothy Keller and Marcel Just discovered that reading cultivates the production of new white matter in the brain.
>
> White matter is composed of nerve fibers, which connect nerve cells to one another throughout the brain. What's more, these white matter nerve cells connect every area of the brain together, helping to transmit signals from one part to another...
>
> Myelin is also responsible for speeding up the transmission of signals from one part of the brain to

another... reading cultivates the production of new white matter. Because white matter consists of cells coated in myelin, which facilitate speedy communication between cells... [and] therefore helps your brain work faster.

When you read, your brain creates new memories, forming new synapses between your brain's nerve cells necessary for the transmission of information from one cell to others, while strengthening neural pathways that already exist. This means that if you read, you should be able to access a greater array of information stored in your memory, and you should also be able to retrieve (or recall) this information more quickly too.[9]

Reading is one of the best uses of your time in both preparing to become a leader and throughout your leadership journey.

Meet with Leaders

In addition to reading widely, you can also learn by having discussions with those in leadership positions around you, including managers, supervisors, and administrators. I recall learning how to do a job from the business owners and community members I worked with. Each person had their own managerial style. Some explained things patiently and answered my questions kindly. Others assumed I would learn how to do things by watching them or other employees. A few would demonstrate the process to ensure I understood it or assign another employee to show me how to do the job.

As an employee, I've witnessed others around me giving orders or training employees. Many leaders made their expectations clear; others were vague and confused new trainees. I learned much about the type of leader I wanted to be as well as the kind I didn't want to be.

If you haven't interacted much with leaders in your job experience, here are suggestions for developing professional relationships:

- Join a committee and study the chairperson's actions
- Request feedback on your work from a respected colleague
- Meet with a mentor for job advice.

Learn through observation, discussion, and, when applicable, imitation.

In "Good Leaders Are Good Learners," research indicated that "leaders who are *in learning mode* develop stronger leadership skills than their peers."[10] The article explains a study that suggests one of the best learning strategies is when leaders acknowledge they don't know something: "I need to learn how to..." They might want to know how to become more convincing or be willing to take more risks. In response to the objective, these individuals look for ways to experiment with alternate methods. One way to become more convincing might be to make more eye contact. The third step of the process is to evaluate the results of the changes that resulted. Individuals must be willing to admit the outcome was not the one they wanted and try something different.

As a group member of a unit or a team, you will have opportunities to observe leadership in action. Analyze the leader's willingness to take a risk and accept responsibility. Observe the leader's response to failure and decide if that is a desirable model to follow. Review meeting minutes to note proposed tasks, then study the results to see how well the process worked. You can make decisions about your future actions in response to the leader's approach to tackling a problem and its outcome.

A boss who is willing to listen can serve as a powerful role model. If your supervisor is approachable, you may be able to schedule meetings to discuss issues of concern or to suggest changes that could enhance your department's efficiency. But one who seems preoccupied or uninterested in your ideas may become an example of what not to do when you step into a leader's role.

Mentors

In his article, "3 Reasons All Great Leaders Have Mentors (and Mentees)," Brian Rashid points out that many globally-renowned leaders have had good coaching: "Steve Jobs had Bill Campbell as a mentor; Mark Zuckerberg had Steve Jobs; Bill Gates had Warren Buffett. Hopefully, I've successfully convinced you that you are never too successful to need a mentor."[11] There is always someone before you who is leading the way and someone following who will learn from your example.

You may already have a mentoring relationship in your upwards trajectory toward leadership. If so, hopefully, it is a positive experience. If it isn't a productive partnership, find another mentor. Today's companies often assign mentors to new employees to help them in their new position. Although mentoring is not a formal process for all organizations, some companies provide this type of support for new employees seeking help from seasoned workers. You could suggest the addition of a mentoring program at your organization if one does not already exist.

Mentoring has become popular as a training tool to help newly hired employees get acclimated to their workplace.

The new employee can learn about the position, the company environment, and institutional policies. From office protocol to water cooler gossip, a mentor can help someone become acquainted with the company and adapt quickly and smoothly.

Having a knowledgeable source available to answer questions and clarify procedures reduces stress and saves time for everyone involved. Often companies issue a mentoring handbook or checklist to direct the process. Other organizations allow the mentoring relationship to unfold naturally with a long-term employee reaching out to help someone new become acclimated.

With the help of a qualified mentor, a new employee often quickly adjusts to the new position. Having a support person who can train, advise, direct, or coach is a valuable service that can make a new employee feel welcome and secure. Not only is this a great form of personal support, but it also facilitates company operations to get the new hire up to speed as soon as possible to save the organization time and money.

This is another company perk that directly or indirectly adds a building block to the leadership training process in a natural, organic style.

Accountability Partner

Many professionals who are seeking transparency find an accountability partner. This will be someone they know well, typically a close friend or business associate, who they can keep informed of the growth or struggles in their work life. Varying levels of self-reporting occur in these relationships. Some individuals trust an accountability partner with intimate details, such as distrust of a coworker. Others prefer to report the main events that serve as benchmarks for progress or setbacks.

You may meet with your accountability partner weekly or monthly in person, by phone, or through a digital medium like Skype. You might have breakfast or jog at the park. Although the time together can be relaxed and friendly, it also provides an opportunity for sharing updates. The focus might be on a specific area, such as using budgeting software, or the focus could be broader, such as clear communication. An accountability partner might suggest objectives or action steps.

A professional accountability relationship may include an individual or a group. Arrangements can be organized by the company during work or take place outside the work schedule and location. You could work with someone on a casual basis or hire a professional accountability partner – someone like a career coach or a licensed therapist.

After the first few sessions, you may decide the partner or group is not the best fit for your needs. Assess the situation to see if it is because of personality differences or if the structure runs counter to your expectations. To be accountable, you must be consistent. If you feel that you are slipping away from your original commitment, speak up, as recommended in this excerpt from an *Inc.com* article by Marissa Levin:

> Comfort leads to complacency. As soon as your accountability falls off your priority list, you owe it to yourself and your group or partner to own that. Life sometimes gets in the way and derails us from moving forward. If this is happening, have the conversation about it. Otherwise, those that have come to depend on you will be disappointed, and resentment will creep in.
>
> It's always best to be honest when you want to disengage, rather than trying to fake your way through your commitment.[12]

You may want to work with another accountability arrangement or hold off to explore other resources. Now that you are aware of this tool, you can pursue it at any stage of your career to determine your readiness for a leadership role.

Working with others to solve problems and meet goals is a proven strategy. That is why group projects are often successful – they combine each person's strengths while overcoming individual weaknesses.

Find colleagues or friends who have the knowledge you are seeking. Establish learning objectives to master related to your career path and leadership goals, such as supervision, management, and administration. Collaborating with people you know, trust, and respect can make the learning curve more navigable.

Leadership means taking the lead and directing the path. We know that business has tricky and challenging roads to navigate. The leader must be ready to forge the path. The leader will confront the first signs of risk or danger and make strategic decisions for an action plan by working with those under his or her purview. Taking the lead is not always glorious or easy. In fact, being courageous often leads into the deepest, darkest trenches where no one else wants to go.

That is why preparing for a leadership role is essential. You may have met people with a natural charisma that draws others to them and enables them to wield influence. But meaningful leadership requires experience that contributes to knowledge, which in turn leads to wisdom.

As acquired knowledge begins to accrue, your next step is to connect with experts. An effective life coach, mentor, or accountability partner might offer the following:

- Focused listening
- Answering questions

- Challenging your assumptions and suggesting alternate perspectives
- Offering encouragement and inspiration
- Issuing cautions and warnings
- Providing guidance and direction.

Like the other tools discussed thus far, this strategy does not come with a financial cost. It is a free give-and-take service.

Education and Training

Up to this point, we have looked at how you can take the initiative toward identifying career objectives and meeting your leadership goals. There are things you can do to establish a career plan and chart your progress with little to minimal cost.

We've considered individuals you can partner with to become professionally astute and accountable. You can choose someone you have known for a long time or approach a person who seems like a viable candidate for becoming a mentor. You might prefer being part of a group rather than working with one person.

You can decide which steps to take as well as when and how. If you want to take a team approach with more people, you will have to coordinate schedules to align with everyone's abilities and availability.

When you have done everything you can on your own or with the help of a mentor or an accountability group, it is time to think about more advanced training. This can take various forms, depending on where you are on your career journey and which skills you are seeking to develop. In the remainder of this chapter, we will look at options to give you a broad vista of training and educational opportunities that can equip you with specific leadership skills. While most readers will not require all of these, some may help you consider what you need to develop your potential and be recognized for your professional competence and potential.

High School Diploma (or GED)

Achieving high school graduation is the first firm step toward advancing to a professional position. Although success has been achieved without this degree, most businesses require the foundational diploma for employment with potential for growth. High school graduates often obtain entry-level positions in companies where they can eventually progress to higher-level jobs.

Trish, a high school graduate, wasn't sure she could afford college. She was hired as a receptionist at an insurance office, earning a little more than the minimum wage. But after a year, her supervisor was impressed by the quality of Trish's work and offered to reimburse her college tuition if she wanted to earn credentials that would enable her to sell insurance. Trish gladly accepted and gained her insurer's license. For Trish, high school provided the foundation on which to build her career. After college graduation, her natural leadership abilities enabled her to open her own successful office.

Training Certificate

Anyone can take training classes on a job-related subject if they meet the enrollment criteria. Often employers will provide expert training for new or long-term employees. The session can be as short as a couple of hours or half a day to a duration of weeks to meet the training objectives. Topics can range from general issues, like becoming an active listener, to deeper concerns, like diversity and inclusion.

Earning a certificate in any professional skill will enhance your resume. In time, you may get the opportunity to take leadership-oriented training. If you have the time, especially for online training that is compatible with your schedule, it may help expedite your career by completing workshops, seminars, and classes in critical topics that could enhance your job performance.

College: Associate Degree

Earning a two-year associate degree at college level can be a significant step forward in your current position. Most organizations recognize the effort required to earn a college degree while simultaneously working and managing other responsibilities. An associate degree takes an in-depth, focused approach to a certain job, such as substance abuse treatment or radiation technology.

An associate degree is usually awarded in general studies or arts and sciences. The degree accomplishes two things:

1. Demonstrates a broad-based perspective on life and work
2. Reveals commitment to self-improvement and learning.

Given the choice of job applicants that includes one having an associate degree versus the others having no college study, employers typically prefer to hire someone with a two-year degree.

University: Bachelor's Degree

Although anyone can be self-taught or hire a tutor to learn business and communication skills, there is really no substitute for a well-rounded college education. Proficiency in math or accounting, verbal and written communication, and managerial strategies can immediately sharpen leadership potential. An educated workforce contributes to higher productivity for the company and greater satisfaction for the employee, especially if financial rewards result. Employees who complete the four years of coursework required for a bachelor's degree often become eligible for company rewards and promotions. Workers might advance from an entry-level position to an administrative role or supervisory job in a few years.

In 2015, the US Department of Education published a *Fact Sheet: Focusing Higher Education on Student Success*. It indicated that a college education was more important but also more expensive than ever:

- College graduates with a *bachelor's degree typically earn 66 percent more* than those with only a high school diploma and are also far less likely to face unemployment.

- Over the course of a lifetime, the average worker with a bachelor's degree will *earn approximately $1 million more* than a worker without a postsecondary education.

- By 2020, an estimated two-thirds of job openings will require postsecondary education or training.[13] Not everyone needs a college degree to become successful in their career field, but certain occupations favor applicants who have earned an associate or bachelor's degree.

Graduate Degrees

Employees in highly specialized occupations may be expected or required by their companies to earn graduate degrees, such as a master's or doctorate diploma or a law degree. High-ranking bank officers may hold a law degree or an MBA – Master of Business Administration. Completing graduate program requirements and earning the degree is not only deeply satisfying on a personal level but also meaningful as well as lucrative at the professional level.

Earning the so-called terminal degree in an occupational field can move someone to the top of their game. It is the slam dunk of the professional world in an academic sense. Of course, not all businesses require formal education at that level, but a graduate degree may be a game-changer that could take your career to new heights.

Not all managers or leaders have a graduate degree; some don't even have a bachelor's degree or an associate degree. But those who obtain academic credentials typically see added opportunities for better-paying jobs with the potential for advancement. College might be the bridge that takes you from a mediocre job to one that fills your work life with interest and meaning.

You will have to decide if investing the time and money in a college diploma will be worth the effort. It might help to talk to your supervisor or a human resource representative to see whether going to college will directly and significantly impact your career progress. It is important to weigh the effort and expense with expected outcomes to decide if college could enhance your career and prepare you for eventual leadership roles.

There are countless ways to expand your knowledge and skills as you prepare to become a leader. Sometimes people don't plan to lead, but circumstances place them in that position. Other times the desire to take charge blossoms over time. Be prepared when opportunity knocks. The more you accomplish in professional development, the readier you will be when an opportunity knocks.

Now that you know more about professional growth options, think about those that interest you. As you decide if you have what it takes to lead others, you can consider the strategies in this chapter as stepping stones toward your ultimate leadership goals.

These basic personal choices can help you better understand your attitude toward future leadership. Getting to know your intrinsic abilities and developing skills will equip you for the path you choose to follow. Then when a leadership opportunity beckons, you can respond with confidence.

Chapter 4

Build Workplace Relationships

As we consider the practical and natural steps you can take to prepare for leadership in your career or the community, this chapter covers ways you can establish your niche at work as you demonstrate your capabilities and interact with colleagues. Since each personality and each organization is different, you will need to find the approach that works best for you.

While working at various companies over the years, I have seen that while businesses have similarities, each is unique. I cannot advise you specifically on how to build your profile at your current job, but I can share what I've learned about becoming the best employee I can be in preparation for a future leadership role. Just as actors must rehearse their lines before filming a movie or enacting a play, a leader-in-training needs to understand how a leader behaves and demonstrate the ability to follow their example.

In the first three chapters, we explored your personal interests to help you find a meaningful and rewarding career. You've read about personal tips and tools for observation, introspection, and reflection. In this chapter, we will look at ways of becoming the employee others admire and follow naturally. When the opportunity comes, you will have the credentials and support to apply for a leadership position.

Leadership styles vary. You might be more reserved than others in your company. You may find it challenging to connect with coworkers when you would rather spend the day at your desk getting things done and directing from a distance.

Yet the importance of face-to-face communication, including video conferencing with tools like Zoom and listening and responding to colleagues and customers, cannot be overstated. Workplace connectivity is critical for building personal and professional relationships in this fast-paced, hectic world. Too often we fail to grasp the meaning of what we hear to be able to respond appropriately. We're too distracted, rushed, or stressed to give close attention to what people say. That can result in problems involving time and cost.

In whatever positions you hold, take steps to prove yourself an analytical person and a staunch supporter of your company's initiatives. Encourage and motivate the people with whom you work. Success stories of renowned leaders resonate with the same refrain – that one individual changed the course of their lives to launch them in a positive direction. Although many people often contribute to our success stories, sometimes one person stands far above the rest in providing support and encouragement when most needed. You might be that person for someone who could use your help.

Listen and Learn: Body Language

In an earlier chapter, we discussed the importance of being a good listener. In this chapter, let's start with body language. Nonverbal communication, such as facial expressions, bodily stances, gestures, and movements, reveals clues about a person's thoughts and feelings. When your boss calls you into her office for an unplanned meeting, you look for hints by how she sits, the expression on her face, and what her hands are doing. Your first impression can impact what you say. If she is in a good mood, you can relax and respond in a lighthearted, confident way. But if your supervisor appears frustrated or angry, you might consciously or unconsciously retreat verbally and emotionally to wait out the storm.

A friend, Jane, was called to an unexpected meeting with her supervisor. Surprised, Jane e-mailed to ask the purpose but was given a vague response. When Jane went to her boss's cubicle at the appointed time, she was stunned to see an administrator there as well. Sensing an ominous atmosphere and feeling like she had been summoned to the principal's office without knowing why, Jane could immediately recognize tension in their quiet demeanors. Jane's impression was accurate. She was asked about workplace actions from a year before, although she had not been given the issue in advance to prepare for the meeting. Fortunately, Jane remained calm and recalled the reason for her actions, which were accepted by her boss and the administrator.

One of my former coworkers, Steve, revealed that he had noticed a colleague, Jeff, looking gloomy and asked if anything was wrong. The colleague admitted feeling disappointed because his work schedule prevented him from joining his widowed mother's eightieth birthday celebration with family in Florida. Steve offered to trade shifts so Jeff could attend the gala, even though Steve's salary contract meant he would work the extra shift without pay. Jeff told others in the department about Steve's kindness, which led to Steve being praised and admired by coworkers, although that was not Steve's intention. Reading the clues in someone's body language can prepare you to read between the lines and respond accordingly.

Don't Ignore Anyone

A caring leader takes time to listen to others and respond thoughtfully, including employees who work at a lower pay grade. Support staff play a key role in company success. Secretaries and assistants can open doors to their supervisors when you need access to those people. Technical and maintenance staff make the work environment clean and safe, as well as technologically functional. Showing appreciation for their work will contribute to a harmonious and collegial work setting.

As you listen to what a coworker has to say, you will build trust and respect within the ranks. Being a sounding board for someone struggling with a job issue will make both of you feel better. Your willingness to share a coworker's burden will be remembered and shared with others. Small acts of kindness serve as paving stones on your leadership journey.

Earlier, we discussed the importance of thoughtful listening to role models and mentors as well as other professional influences. This type of listening might be called *passive listening*, as you absorb knowledge without necessarily doing anything with it.

However, *active listening* entails action to strengthen the ways in which you reinforce and process added information: repeating, questioning, note-taking, and restating. Instead of simply hearing what someone says, think about what you have heard and decide how to use that information either now or by storing it in your memory for the future. Interaction with the speaker during a conversation or later for clarity may be necessary.

At work and in other arenas of life, you will be tempted to tune out a speaker with whom you disagree or whose delivery is unimpressive. But an effective leader pays attention to the speaker to understand their perspective. Depending on the situation, you may need to correct something the speaker has said or request an explanation or details for something you did not understand. Don't just ignore the fact that the person's message is unclear. Mistakes and problems occur when communication falters.

Sometimes executives send short e-mail summaries of meetings addressed to all participants and invite their feedback on the key points. Everyone can contribute to the discussion and establish agreement on matters covered. The edited draft will be recirculated as a formal or informal record of the proceedings and will be given to everyone involved as well as maintained on file. As stated earlier, written records of important discussions or meetings provide a reliable record for future reference.

We all know that gossip and rumors can spread throughout a company and damage someone's reputation. It's never a good idea to become part of the rumor mill. That's why it is essential to listen carefully to the official information, be sure you understand the intended message, and follow up with questions if needed. Company records are kept confidential and should not be shared with other employees who are not affected by the communication.

Should a manager (or leader) respond to office gossip or ignore it?

An article titled "How to Deal With Difficult People at Work" urges action to be taken if gossip results in situations like these:

- Disrupting the workplace and the business of work
- Hurting employees' feelings
- Damaging interpersonal relationships
- Injuring employee motivation and morale

Author Susan Heathfield claims managers who ignore problematic gossip "can destroy a department." She urges managers to address gossip in the same way as other employee infractions by following company protocols like issuing a verbal warning, a written reprimand, and any disciplinary action that might be needed – and finally, firing the employee if gossip continues. Failure to do so can diminish employee morale and cause them to lose confidence in their leader.[14]

Reflect on What You Hear (or Read)

Have you ever sent an e-mail response and then realized you misunderstood the sender's message to which you were responding? It's not only embarrassing to send an inaccurate reply, but it also hurts your credibility. Before responding to an important message, reread it again. Think about the best way to address the issue. Write a draft of your response, review it, revise it, and then send it when you are satisfied that you have provided an effective response.

Without the bonus clues of body language, facial expressions, and voice intonations, along with the opportunity to interact with the speaker in dialogue, you will need to pay extra attention to the phone conversation or written message you've received.

In today's busy world, we are eager to clear our desks of tasks awaiting attention. In a rush to respond, you might send a message that overlooks key points referenced in the message you received. The communication process is delayed when the recipient of your answer must contact you for details that your response missed. Not only does that slow the communication cycle and hinder productivity, but it also may place you in a questionable position of not being a careful listener or reader and not paying adequate attention to information from others. As a reputable leader, your communication skills should be professionally evident at all times.

Reflection is lacking today. We need to set aside time for thoughtful reflection on important concerns. The *Merriam-Webster Dictionary* offers several definitions of "reflection," of which two fit our purpose:

> 6: a thought, idea, or opinion formed, or a remark made as a result of meditation
> 7: consideration of some subject matter, idea, or purpose

These definitions point to the notion of mindfully evaluating information and ideas.

Dr. Susan Madsen explores the roots of reflection in contemporary business. Based on her experience as a speaker, coach, consultant, and writer, she advocates the importance of deep reflection for leaders and managers:

> Individuals cannot truly develop as leaders unless they are receptive to continuous and deep learning. In fact, learning is at the core of effective leadership development, and deep learning is the process through which we can use our experiences to transform. Through this type of learning, we fundamentally change the way we see ourselves, others, and the world around us. This deliberate action is known as "transformational learning."
>
> One of the essential elements of this deep and transformational learning is called critical reflection. According to scholars, self-reflection comes not just from thinking about one's experiences; it also requires you to examine the underlying beliefs and assumptions that influence how you make sense of those experiences.[15]

Setting aside time to think about what you hear or read is one of the most important things a leader can do. In fact, surveys of executives report a high number of them spend the bulk of most workdays reading and writing. The opposite approach would be to rush a memo or speak offhand without complete details or a clear understanding of the matter.

Catherine Ducharme, a certified coach, speaker, and the co-founder of Fluency Leadership, posted a LinkedIn article about the importance of reflection in business communication:

> I remember early in my career being asked to write an article on a complex topic. I had few details and little direction. I did my research and poured my heart into it only to have it completely re-written, except for one sentence the manager saw fit to use. I had clearly missed the mark but wasn't sure how or why, not even after reading the final version. I felt inadequate as a writer and that I had let my manager down. I came to realize the failure was not my writing skills but that I had no idea what the expectations were, and I got no feedback or corrective coaching. It was a missed opportunity to learn...
>
> Self-reflection starts with leading with the assumption of generosity which, as Brené Brown describes, is believing that people are doing the best that they can. It also requires us to trust the team we've hired, hold them capable, and commit to developing and coaching them to success.[16]

We discussed reflection earlier in this book to help readers find ways of digesting and processing valuable impressions. Here, you are encouraged to reflect at work on the infor-

Build Workplace Relationships

mation shared with you for a purpose. When you practice self-reflection, you honor the time and trust offered by coworkers and others who express ideas that are important to them. Some questions for reflection:

- Do I completely understand this message (speech, dialogue, e-mail)?
- What questions do I have?
- What further information is needed?
- Is it clear what the person wants or expects, and am I the best person to provide it?

On reflection, trivial details may become known that will change your understanding of the issues as well as your response.

As you continue to develop workplace skills and prepare for leadership, being recognized as an effective listener will gain the respect and admiration of others. You will be seen as someone who cares about others' ideas and listens to what they say before responding casually or rendering a judgment. A thoughtful leader is valued over one who is rash or careless.

Establish Your Niche

As you start building your leadership profile to apply for managerial positions, include experience from areas of your life that demonstrate applicable skills. Update your resume with relevant life experience that has been or could be applied in the workplace.

For example, list the areas in which you support your community. As a full-time employee, you may not have time for much involvement. But you might be doing more than you realize:

- Youth sports coach
- Community fundraiser
- County fair sponsor
- Volunteer
- Recycling coordinator
- Charity event organizer
- Civic or business group member
- House of worship leader (music, drama, study groups, etc.)

There are additional ways in which you donate time, talent, or resources to your community. Helping with field trips at your children's school or cleaning up a local park are two examples.

Next, consider the specific duties you perform in community service. Maybe you spearheaded a fundraiser for a family struggling to pay for medical treatments they cannot afford. Or you might serve as the treasurer of a civic group such as Rotary or a sports club. You may be surprised to take an inventory of your experience and find that you have learned or developed skills that can be used at work and possibly in a leadership role.

In your company of employment, opportunities to lead will depend on your current position as well as your organization's structure. A smaller company might have an unexpected need for supervisory assistance if the owner gets busy or must be away for a time. In a larger business, you could be asked to fill in temporarily for an open position until a new employee can be hired. Or you may notice that a department is short-handed and offer help. When you do an excellent job, you will be remembered as someone who is dependable, helpful, and competent in your short-term stint. You may be offered more short-term roles that will increase your leadership experience, complement your resume, and enhance the possibility of being considered for a full-time leadership position.

Should you offer to lead an initiative or wait to be asked? If you have been employed at the company for a while, you probably have a sense of when to speak up. Someone who believes in your ability to lead might let you know of an upcoming need. You might be familiar with a department where leadership is lacking. You can also ask your supervisor about leadership needs that may be developing.

From a practical standpoint, the following ideas can help you prepare for those unexpected opportunities:

- Get to know how the company works. As you assess the organizational structure, you will begin to understand the leader's role in each unit and consider where you might fit in if an opening should occur.

- Examine available job descriptions for lead roles in the company. If you are unable to do that, discreetly find out what the leaders do in their areas, including who they supervise and their usual responsibilities.

- Identify temporary needs for leaders or new positions that may become available. Find out what those positions will require in terms of education, experience, and skills.

- Review your job description to find connections between what you currently do and what leaders do in their positions.

- Identify gaps in your work history and weak or missing

skills that need to be addressed in preparation for leadership. For example, if the position of authority you want requires basic Spanish skills, take a Spanish class or two.

- Look for unidentified needs in positions of authority. You might notice that a manager in a specific unit is not conducting annual performance reviews. Learn how to conduct a performance review by examining online models or reading books on organizational management. If qualified, offer your assistance to the current manager. When a position for a manager in that unit opens, you will have the necessary skill.

- Study different managerial styles at your workplace. Decide which one(s) best suit your background and work style. Cultivate that style through online resources and business books and resources. If possible, informally job shadow someone in the position of interest to see if you would be a good fit someday.

As your understanding improves of the leadership options that eventuate, update your resume with new leadership abilities for when the call comes. Even a temporary position can increase your visibility as a valuable employee with leadership potential.

Now that you have developed a leadership profile through an aptitude assessment, skills training, and community involvement, as well as workplace skill building, you are ready to develop a niche. Although you don't need to specialize in just one type of leadership skill, such as organization or finances, it helps to have valid experience that you can point to during an interview. Emphasize job duties that have equipped you to motivate employees or develop a promising initiative. Cultivating a leadership niche establishes you as an expert, and companies love to hire, nurture, and promote expertise!

Be Supportive

How does your company support employees' need for training, motivation, or promotion? Are you involved in that process as a mentor or trainer? If not, you can actively support your colleagues by sharing your skills in offering a training session if your company approves it. If you are unable to serve as an expert trainer, look for ways to use your skills to fill company or employee needs.

You could be the person who organizes informal employee gatherings over lunch, after work, or for holidays and special events. You can suggest casual meetings to help everyone adjust to upcoming operating changes or to discuss the implications of a policy change. These gatherings can be as productive, or more so, as officially scheduled meetings.

Another way to connect with your coworkers and build camaraderie is through social media. However, you must be careful to display professional behavior when using platforms like these:

- LinkedIn
- Instagram
- Facebook
- Twitter
- TikTok

Some are more for fun and personal use. LinkedIn is a professional networking site for people wanting to share ideas and look for jobs. Although there is much more to this site, it is designed primarily for business purposes.

As an employee, you do not want to create a separate individual brand. But you can launch your personal brand noncompetitively to enhance your professional credentials.

- Post a brief article or tweet about an issue related to your industry or expertise. Posting occasional articles will attract readers and followers, which builds your profile on social media accounts. For example, if hundreds of viewers repost your marketing tips on LinkedIn, your application for a marketing director position may be stronger as a result.

- Comment on other people's posts. You can also like or repost them. Supporting members in the online community often boomerangs into building a following for your comments to enhance your profile. Many employers cruise social media to monitor employees (rightly or wrongly). Maintain a positive image in your social media accounts, which impresses others and encourages professional relationships.

Teach a Class

With a college degree, you may be able to teach a class online or on campus at a local college. University affiliation expands your influence and enlarges your expert status. With flexible scheduling options, you could teach an evening or weekend course that won't interfere with your regular job duties. You might also teach online. Make sure you get job clearance if your employer requires it.

Suppose you don't hold a college degree but have earned a

certificate in a skill or ability like medical terminology. In that case, you might be able to teach a workshop or training session at a career center or a technical school. The certificate, in tandem with teaching experience, is likely to boost your resume when applying for a leadership role.

Earning a university-level tutoring certificate is another simple but effective way to establish your expertise in a subject area. Assisting others in a classroom setting or one-to-one private tutoring sessions contributes to your status as an expert. Companies hire applicants or promote employees with this type of experience.

Publish an Article or Book

Becoming a published author is one of the most impressive feats to accomplish. Getting your ideas in print and building readership shows that the public endorses your credibility and insight.

You can publish a blog about your experiences in a specific occupation. Offer guest posts to similar blogs or those that are high profile in your area of expertise.

Newspapers (print or online) are another publishing route. A newspaper editorial or interview helps underscore your reputation as an insider in the topic field. Writing for a trade publication also attracts interest in your experience and skills and identifies you as someone who is aware.

Publishing a book could become the pinnacle of success from which to launch your leadership persona. Before you say, "I could never do that," be assured that you can write and publish a meaningful book that others will find interesting and useful. A published book establishes you as an expert, and expert status helps define you as a leadership candidate. Here are basic tips for publishing a book in your area of expertise:

- Organize your ideas on a topic related to your experience. You might want to author a book about grappling with the challenges of transitioning from blue-collar to white-collar work, for example. A nonfiction how-to book should explore a problem and provide a realistic solution.

    You might prefer to author a book about meeting life's challenges that will inspire others to follow a similar path to success. Maybe you come from an immigrant family who faced obstacles in their quest for survival in their new country. Readers love books based on real life. Choose a focus you know a great deal about and organize how you will present the information, usually described in a synopsis (summary) or a chapter outline.

- Write a draft of the book manuscript. It may take months or years. Alternatively, you can hire a ghostwriter for assistance in preparing the book for publication.

- Hire a professional editor to review the manuscript and correct the errors. An editor can also enhance the flow and improve the style. You can do these tasks yourself, if you have strong grammar skills and professional writing experience.

- Compare publishing options. Self-publishing is growing in popularity, and some of these companies produce high-quality books that are enthusiastically embraced by the public.

    Amazon's Kindle Direct Publishing program will help you launch a publication-ready manuscript electronically or in print format. They provide sample book covers and help you find an editor if needed. In return, authors sign an agreement sharing book sale profits by percentage, with more than one option to choose from. The books become available in countries around the world. However, you will need a marketing plan to promote the book and attract buyers. Kindle's program offers promotional options.

- Obtain a manuscript review from a self-publishing company that has a strong track-record of positive feedback from satisfied authors. Professional writing assistance from a qualified team of publishing professionals can help polish and complete your book.

- Submit the manuscript to a conventional publisher. You might need the assistance of an agent, with rates ranging from 10 percent to 15 percent for their representation to publishers who will not otherwise consider your book. A publisher's review may take weeks to months.

- When your book is published, request reviews to be posted at book-selling websites like Amazon and Barnes & Noble. You should also market your book to libraries, certain types of related businesses, and schools that might use it as a textbook. You may want to participate in book signings that attract fans seeking an autographed copy.

Publishing a book involves creative marketing and collaboration skills that complement your work experience and job training. Employers often give published authors greater consideration since a published book enhances your job credentials through life experience and strong writing skills, along with publisher and reader approbation.

Make a Presentation

Speaking to a crowd, whether at work or in public, establishes you as an expert. On the job, you may be qualified to lead a training session or give a motivational speech for a company-wide initiative led by your department. Look for ways to share your ideas and enthusiasm at work

Outside the company, arrange your expertise into a presentation of about 20 to 30 minutes. Organize a PowerPoint demonstration to accompany the session. You can use other visual aids as well, but make sure they work properly and convey the material clearly to the audience.

If you recently traveled abroad, you could prepare a talk about the highlights of your trip. As a company representative, you might be able to explain a new product or process that will soon be available to the community. Always dress for the occasion and convey a positive, upbeat attitude.

Public presentations by authors often include the option of selling their books following the event. If you publish a book, you can usually buy copies at a discount and sell them for whatever price you wish. Keep receipts for income tax purposes. Many buyers will request an autographed copy. If time permits, it's nice to include a brief personalized message by adding "Best wishes" or "Nice meeting you" on the blank first page or title page, whichever the buyer prefers.

A book that sells 5,000 copies is moderately successful. Most first-time authors without a professional or celebrity platform will not sell. Over time, however, sales may increase as the book's publicity ramps up. You can pay a marketing expert to help promote the book by scheduling radio, TV, and Internet interviews and presentations if you have the time and interest.

As shown throughout the first part of this book, there are dozens of practical ways, simple and free or affordable, to reinforce your managerial knowledge and pave the way on your journey toward leadership. Many people are offered the unexpected opportunity to lead, so be ready when the time comes.

If leadership is your goal or gift, start preparing. You may need to lead your community or company at a future point. You don't have to spend tons of money to learn how to lead. Follow your instincts and use what you have been given or earned.

Chapter 5

Be Positive

Have you ever had a boss who motivated you to do your best work? Was it someone with a firm sense of purpose? Or maybe a manager highlighted your mistakes and insisted on improvement?

The best boss I have had was an administrator in an office where I held an assistant position for five years. He was kind, patient, and honest about my strengths and weaknesses. I could count on him to point out my flaws while praising my successes. He never raised his voice or issued threats. Nor did he make promises that he didn't keep. In fact, one of the best things I recall about this man was his efforts to help me reach my potential and beyond to attain a higher role in the organization. Although I didn't always agree with his decisions affecting clients, his ethics were solid. He became a role model who believed in me before I believed in myself.

Each of us has a different personality that influences our approach to work. Many jobs depend on interpersonal relationships with decision-makers, coworkers, and support staff, so you need a communication style that will fit your present job and prepare you for future leadership roles.

In this chapter, we are adding to your professional development toolkit by underscoring the importance of a positive mindset. Ironically, like a self-fulfilling prophecy, how we view our circumstances tends to influence their outcome. If you complain, feel stressed, and don't feel committed to your job, there's a good chance you won't keep it. Or if you do, you are unlikely to feel fulfilled and do the best work of which you are capable.

If you consistently look for the good aspects of your work situation, however, you have a strong chance of feeling contented and performing high-quality work.

Practice Positivity

While none of us can be happy all the time, we can make an effort to manifest a cheerful spirit at work for the sake of others as well as ourselves. Several research studies have linked a positive attitude to better mental and physical health. A healthy employee – physically, mentally, and emotionally – is a more effective employee.

Robyn Whalen's blog post, titled "7 Tips for Promoting Positivity in Your Workplace," claims that "Practicing positivity and optimism has been linked to numerous health benefits, increased productivity, and less stress." Two simple ways of accomplishing this are to practice gratitude and to smile![17]

What's special about smiling? No one wants to look like a grinning fool, but there are benefits to letting your lips convey a sense of well-being.

An article in *Psychology Today*, "Smiling: Why It's Important in Your Personal Life and Workplace," explains numerous benefits of smiling:

> A smile is contagious, medicinal, therapeutic, relaxes our muscles, and even makes us look more pleasant and approachable. When it becomes a habit to show pleasantness to another person through a smile, noth-

ing in the world can take it away from you, even the daily challenges of life. A healthy smile is inviting and invigorating and can motivate people to reciprocate with their smiles, whether in a social setting or professional sphere.[18]

Scientific research reveals that smiling, even when you are alone, can lift your spirits because the movement of your mouth muscles sends a "happy" message to your brain. The same technique applies when you smile at others but don't feel particularly upbeat. Going through the motions of smiling is a simple, cost-free way to experience greater satisfaction immediately and elicit a similar response from others.

Choosing the "high road" of a positive nature over criticism and sulking will make you feel happier and enhance how you interact with others. You don't have to give pricey gifts or walk around shaking hands with everyone to create a harmonious work environment. Be pleasant while doing your job. Start with a pleasant smile, add a few choice words of encouragement or praise, and you will brighten someone's day as well as your own. These are simple things we can and should do every day at home or on the job.

Longstanding research shows that the physical act of smiling, even without positive emotions behind it, can enhance your mood and improve your outlook. An article titled "What Research Tells Us About When (and When Not) to Smile at Work" describes the chemical response to the act of smiling:

> At work there are a combination of powerful biological and evolutionary forces. At the neurological level, smiling is said to spur a chemical reaction in the brain, releasing dopamine, which increases happiness, and serotonin, which reduces stress. At the same time,

we're culturally conditioned from birth to associate smiling with happiness.[19]

Of course, it shouldn't be a fake smile, or your coworkers will question your authenticity. Nor should it be a mysterious Cheshire Cat smile, causing those around you to wonder what you're thinking. A sincere, even brief, Mona Lisa-type grin is adequate for putting people at ease and lightening the atmosphere. And that impact comes from just one basic muscle group in the body!

There is a whole field of research devoted to the study and analysis of body language, and it is fascinating to discover what your facial expressions, hand gestures, and general stance reveal about your mood or intentions. Here are basic tips to keep in mind regarding what your positive bodily movements, intentional or otherwise, suggest to those around you.

Space

Body language experts claim there are various bubble sizes of space around each of us that determine our comfort level when speaking with others. Typically, two to three feet is about the closest most professionals will tolerate someone's proximity to them, except for a whispered comment at a loud gathering, for example. Six feet is common for general conversation. Anything more distant might make it difficult to communicate easily or clearly if the environment is noisy or busy.

Eyes

Look directly at someone to whom you are speaking. Frequently glancing sideways or downwards can make you appear distracted. However, you don't need to stare to show you are listening. Your body should be facing that person during the conversation rather than turning away or walking past, except for very casual interactions. Avoid holding a prolonged gaze; a couple of seconds is usually effective. When you smile, let it reach your eyes to show sincerity.

Hands

Keep your hands relaxed while talking to coworkers. Occasional hand gestures are fine if you don't overdo them. Avoid tackling other tasks simultaneously, like checking your phone or picking lint off your jacket. When necessary, multitasking is a valuable skill, but try not to multitask when conversing with coworkers or customers, which can make them feel unvalued.

It's best not to touch others unless you have a close relationship with them or know they won't mind. Shaking hands, a pat on the arm, or a quick hug might be acceptable to non-coworkers or someone you haven't seen in a while but be aware of intercultural social customs to avoid unintentional offense. For example, in certain traditional cultures of the Middle East and Asia, you should avoid touching a female or giving her special attention unless she is a relative or embraces Western social practices.

Feet

Point your feet toward the person with whom you are having a dialogue. Our bodies tend to face the way our feet point as if preparing to move in that direction. Directly facing someone shows genuine interest and not a hurried or forced interaction. Try not to tap your toes if the conversation drags or you become impatient; excuse yourself politely and leave if you must. Similarly, when seated with legs crossed, avoid swinging or pumping either or both legs, as this suggests anxiety or restlessness.

Voice

In addition to choosing words carefully, be aware of your vocal intonation. We all know that rising intonation conveys a question: "You're scheduling the meeting for *Thursday*?" or "*You're* scheduling the meeting for Thursday?" Otherwise, the statement could be heard as a fact: "You're scheduling the meeting for Thursday." (There might be a slight drop in tone at the end of the sentence to signal a statement rather than a question.)

A loud voice is not usually required at work unless you work in a noisy area. Modulate your tone to be polite rather than controlling and to display confidence without arrogance. Be aware of the tone of your voice when you are irritable or annoyed. Emotions can show through the sound of your voice as much as in the words. The same idea can be applied to the risk of showing favoritism. If your tone drops slightly or becomes boisterous when speaking about an employee, others will sense it from your voice. A soft, gentle tone that departs from your routine, matter-of-face intonation may hint at a preference or soft spot for the person you are talking about. A sharp tone, in contrast, might indicate a less favorable impression of the person you are speaking to or about.

Another positive aspect of voice inflection includes avoiding sarcasm, even in jest. An exception would be when you are speaking casually with someone, and you can break this rule because the person knows you well enough to understand the context and intention. But with people you don't know well or in a more formal situation, maintain a courteous tone with light inflections to keep the exchange interesting and controlled. Use pauses, emphasis, and repetition to achieve a heightened effect, if needed. A pause should typically last about 10–15 seconds to let your words sink in while avoiding an uncomfortably long silence.

What you say is as important as how you say it. Choose your words carefully. In fact, when preparing for a meeting, think about what you will say and the best way to convey the information. While you don't need to memorize a scripted speech, tentatively arrange the points you want to make and potential responses to anticipated issues or questions.

When differences of opinion arise, avoid challenging someone's opinion: "You can't be serious!" or "That isn't right."

Instead, ask questions: "Can you give an example of that?"

Speaking in a comfortable, relaxed tone helps ease an exchange where the topic might unleash differing perspectives and cause tempers to flare.

I remember a nasty confrontation between two employees erupting at a department meeting, making other attendees extremely uncomfortable. The pair of so-called colleagues not only disagreed with and criticized each other over the issue being addressed but also raised their voices and labeled each other disrespectfully. From the looks on everyone's faces – about 30 altogether – emotions ranged from dismay to disgust at this blatant display of unprofessional immaturity and incivility. The tenor of the meeting abruptly turned sour, and it was soon adjourned.

Keep in mind that in group gatherings, whatever you say and how you say it will be shared amongst several people who will apply their own interpretation of the facts and surmise and report accordingly to others. Most professional meetings appoint someone to take "the minutes" of the meeting, that is, to record a summary of key events and the disposition of issues that were discussed. The summary becomes an official record. Some scribes who serve as recorders at the meeting will decide whether to include or exclude unsavory elements. Whether in the meeting minutes or simply forwarded as hearsay, we know how gossip and rumors can distort the facts. Your reputation could be strewn in tatters afterward if you misspeak or your words are misrepresented. Plan for clarity and be succinct when speaking on the record or about prominent issues at work.

These days, anything you say might end up on social media – distorted and misrepresented for all the world to see! Worse, if your boss hears about it, you could end up in trouble, and your leadership goals could be derailed. Employers have been known to cruise social media and reprimand employees for a questionable or critical post that puts the company at risk. If you want to post about your job or coworkers, make a positive comment. It's always a good idea to practice the Golden Rule (paraphrased): Treat others the way you want to be treated.

To apply what we have discussed so far, remember to maintain a pleasant outlook each day, with a smile when feasible, a considerate manner to all, and a cheerful outlook toward the work you do. Yes, tough times may develop during an economic downturn or a company disruption, but a can-do approach demonstrates faith in your colleagues and a commitment to the organization to help keep morale high.

Inclusivity

Many organizations draw from a naturally diverse pool of applicants. Assuming all are equally qualified, it is important to ensure everyone has the same opportunities for employment or promotion when selecting or recognizing employees from their respective pools.

Maybe your company emphasizes inclusivity. Or you may feel that since you do not directly hire or fire employees, the goal of inclusivity does not pertain to you. But you may have more influence than you realize, and you should use it wisely.

For example, organizations typically invite candidates for open positions to get acquainted with company employees in an informal meet-and-greet session. Or the candidates might be asked to provide sample work materials or to conduct a brief meeting with representative employees that can be shared with a larger group of employees. When asked to provide feedback on job applicants, assess their credentials and capabilities fairly and honestly.

It is unethical and illegal to assume that because someone has special needs or is from a certain racial, ethnic, religious, or sexual orientation background, that individual will make a better or worse addition to the company or work more or less efficiently. Apply a reasonable grid – your own or the company's – to evaluate candidates' credentials and performance. When asked to analyze someone's job performance over time, use the same objective criteria.

Employees with integrity never use stereotypical slurs or language, nor do they make baseless assumptions about an individual's potential – or lack of. It is wise to maintain the view that everyone has the right to apply for a position they are qualified to perform and that their ability to do good work will be evaluated fairly. This is a critical way to build trust within an organization and prepare for leadership. If others notice that you hold biases against certain types of people, they may not trust you to be objective in other elements of leadership. Be a leader by promoting inclusivity in whatever ways you can, especially when you assume a leadership role. Susanne Ricee explains, in her blog post titled "What Is Inclusivity?":

> Leaders of institutions, communities, and organizations must be the prime movers of inclusivity in society. Ordinary folks take their cue from them, so they must set a good example for others by taking the lead and initiative in it. And they can take the lead by actively promoting inclusivity by words and deeds.[20]

If your vehicle were hit by another car in a collision that left you paralyzed, would you expect to lose your job? Or would you hope and trust that your employer would find a way to accommodate your new condition so you could maintain your position?

Of course, it is unwise and unethical to practice reverse discrimination or affirmative action that gives anyone with a special or different status extra or undue consideration. An organization should hire employees based on their ability to do a respectable job. Qualified employees with special needs or differing characteristics can be accommodated within reason.

If your organization already has an inclusive approach to hiring, be involved with the process, when possible, by providing balanced feedback on request. If inclusivity is not yet on your company's radar when hiring new employees, you may want to step up and proactively suggest ways of integrating inclusivity and diversity. When colleagues can trust you to stand up for everyone's rights, they will trust you to support their rights when you are in charge. Building trust with your colleagues is an integral part of becoming an effective leader, as indicated in this *Forbes* article which cites Rick Hammel, CEO and founder of Elements Global Services:

Over half of American workers feel they have no one to turn to with a workplace issue, according to previous research. This year has brought even more strife for many companies making tough decisions about staffing, creating new work policies to reflect remote desires, recruiting in a world with fewer willing workers and in some cases shutting down entire organizations.[21]

The article also cites Todd Moran, chief learning strategist at NovoEd:

If inclusion and belonging are the ultimate blocks in the pyramid of employee engagement, open lines of communication between colleagues and managers are the glue holding it all together...[22]

Not only is inclusivity at work the right thing to do, but it also helps establish trust between leaders and employees. By doing your part, coworkers will learn that you stand up for what is right and will ensure that everyone within your purview gets fair consideration.

Mental Health Support

In the past few years, the world has experienced dramatic changes and severe problems that have taken a toll on people's mental and emotional health. The COVID pandemic, the war in Europe, and economic uncertainties have contributed to a steep rise in substance abuse, violent crime, and financial hardships. Public safety has declined, caused by unprovoked assaults on the elderly and the infirm. Confronted with these problems and worries, many employees report higher levels of stress, anxiety, depression, anger, and suicidal thoughts.

While it is not a company's responsibility to address personal issues in employees' lives, managers and leaders should be aware of the mental status and emotional condition of workers on the job. There are things a leader or leader-in-training can do to support coworkers dealing with unrelenting pressures that are taking a toll on their workload and personal life.

A *Harvard Business Review* article, "8 Ways Managers Can Support Employees' Health," points to the escalating problem of employee mental health with a study that was conducted:

> We saw an impact early in the pandemic. At the end of March and in early April, our nonprofit organization, Mind Share Partners, conducted a study of global employees in partnership with Qualtrics and SAP. We found that the mental health of almost 42% of respondents had declined since the outbreak began. Given all that's happened between then and now, we can only imagine that the figure has increased.[23]

The authors suggest that the long-term effects are likely to be even more extensive, and two years later, in 2022, we can verify that mental health issues remain a growing concern.

The good news is the article recommends leaders use their managerial skills to address these problems by being vulnerable and by modeling healthy behaviors. Promoting inclusivity and flexibility, as well as clear and accessible mental health information, is also helpful. Employees should know what type of services the company can offer or refer them to in the local community.

If you are not directly involved in this aspect of employee support, become informed about how it works so that you can advise colleagues who show emotional distress or who ask for your help. Be open to and accepting of coworkers who may feel embarrassed to admit their emotional struggles. You might be able to suggest that the company provide certain types of practical support if they cannot offer professional-level therapeutic or psychological counseling. To give employees a break from job pressure and encourage personal care, organizations are introducing programs like the following:

- Pet programs that bring trained service dogs or cuddly small animals to the workplace for employees to enjoy in a relaxed break room setting.

- Literature circles similar to an informal book club in which employees who wish to participate share a read-aloud time during lunch or break time. Selections range from poetry to inspirational works.

- Exercise areas like an indoor workout room or an outside walking path.

- Onsite massage therapist for shoulder massage one day each week or month.

- Potluck lunches to encourage employees to socialize and relax with one another.

- Weight management group (Weight Watchers, Keto) for health and self-esteem.

Other topics to unite employees might center on interests like photography, nature appreciation, or a project to help the local community.

Naturally, it is left to the discretion of each company to

determine the type and level of support it can offer its employees. But even if you are not a manager or a decision-maker in this process, you can become an advocate for coworkers by suggesting or supporting reasonable efforts by the company to support employees' mental health. At a major university, where a tight budget and uncertain enrollment had everyone's nerves on edge, the psychology professor suggested a "Stress Fest" day. A local ice cream shop donated free milkshakes, and suggestions like those above were scheduled for the day. It was a tremendous success, with many agreeing the event helped relieve recent anxieties.

Although your job keeps you busy, keep an eye on work-life around you. If you notice that a colleague appears to be in distress, consider your options for helping. Depending on your professional relationship with the person, you may be able to ask if everything is okay. If you are aware of an ongoing problem in the coworker's life, such as an abusive relationship or prolonged illness, you might suggest that the person talks to a counselor. If you see evidence of physical harm, such as bruises or black eyes, refer the employee to your HR office director.

If an employee talks about suicide, you may have an ethical and possible legal responsibility to escort that person to a manager's office or the company psychologist, if there is one. Otherwise, you should contact the human resource department while the person is with you to ask what to do. Companies often have a policy for responding to someone who has expressed suicidal thoughts or intentions or a person who confesses a crime or admits to having criminal thoughts of hurting someone. Your company should have clear directives on how to respond to these situations. If there isn't one, ask the HR department to prepare a procedures manual so everyone will know what to do if the scenario should present.

Be Happy

Yes, it sounds like a cliché to say that we're supposed to stay happy at work. None of us is happy every day, all day. But we can mitigate a gloomy or contentious job environment by doing our part. It doesn't take much effort to smile, offer praise or condolences, and extend a helping hand or a listening ear to a coworker in need. You might make a substantial difference in that person's life. In fact, kindness has been shown to change the mind of someone bent on suicide.

If your goal is to one day lead a unit, a department, or a business, you will need to be in touch with your employees' mental health and do what you can to protect their well-being. Start now in your current position to think and act like the leader you are destined to become.

Chapter 6

Establish Integrity

Integrity begins with your approach to managing your job duties. Do you comply with company policies or evade procedures you consider cumbersome or unnecessary? Have you ever taken a shortcut at work to save time or cut costs? Maybe you decided to help someone in a way that didn't quite fit the rules. While your intention is good, the outcome might not be what you hoped.

Dictionary definitions of integrity include the actions of being honest, morally upright, and whole or undivided. Trustworthiness and reliability are two additional ways of thinking about integrity. Coworkers and supervisors will know that you are an employee they can count on to make reasonable and ethical decisions.

A lack of integrity represents the opposite: someone who cannot be trusted to do the right thing for the company or coworkers.

Sometimes we try to do the right things the wrong way. For example, if you feel sick but still go to work to finish a project, your illness could spread to others. If several people come down sick and miss work, the project could be indefinitely delayed. It would have been better to stay home and wait to feel better.

Which Ethics Apply?

A professional communications trainer, Claire, was asked to teach four communications sessions at the mid-size corporation where she worked. With 18 employees enrolled, the sessions would take place at the end of the workday, from 5:00 to 7:00 p.m. Participants would earn a stipend for successfully completing the training designed to enhance their job skills.

At the second session, two enrolled employees asked Claire if they could leave 30 minutes early each session as they were scheduled for a night shift at a second part-time job where they worked, and Claire verified their employment. The employees offered to make up the lost training time on a Saturday, if necessary. The company had previously approved the women's secondary employment but was unaware that the two wanted to leave training early to get to their second job on time. Claire thought about consulting the department manager, but since both employees were doing well with training and agreed to spend extra time studying the materials to catch up, Claire decided to dismiss them early without requesting company approval.

Over the next week, Claire learned that other trainees in her sessions had outside responsibilities: youth sports coaching, birth preparation classes, and family care responsibilities. In the third class, the last hour of training was reserved for writing assignments that Claire would assist with and collect for feedback. To be fair to all who asked to leave early for legitimate reasons, Claire agreed to dismiss those participants early as well, with their agreement to put extra time into completing the assignment. Despite fewer students staying the entire time, Claire received full pay since she had remained in class for the designated sessions with most students.

When the training concluded, most enrollees had met the objectives, except for one who dropped out and another who could not meet the learning objectives. Claire felt the enrollees who had been excused early had completed the training successfully based on classwork and submitted assignments. She decided, however, that in future sessions, she would insist everyone complete the training at the designated time rather than leave early for any reason. If there were competing commitments, employees would be advised to take the training in a subsequent session when their schedules permitted.

About ten months later, during her performance review, the department manager challenged Claire's allowing some enrollees to leave early and revealed that two had complained. Taken aback, since no one had mentioned it previously, Claire explained why she had let students leave early and that she would manage the situation differently in the future. The manager's tone was accusatory and condemning, and Claire felt that her decisions were considered unethical. Although she gave permission to leave early for what she felt were valid reasons, she realized that even well-intentioned decisions could ethically compromise a work commitment and influence others' perceptions of her integrity.

When making decisions at work that affect other people or your work performance, it is important to consider other points of view. You might be able to do a day's work in six-and-a-half hours instead of eight. But if you are paid for eight hours, shouldn't you maintain the requisite conditions or request a pay adjustment?

Ethical dilemmas often include grey areas that cause disagreement. For example, you might feel it's better to give a chronically late employee a strict warning while another manager wants to fire that person. Who's right? Many factors should be considered in major workplace decisions:

- How often has the employee been late?
- Are viable excuses provided – with evidence?
- Is there a way to reasonably resolve the issue?
- Have previous reminders or warnings gone unheeded?

A thoughtful leader must consider all the variables before making a life-changing decision based on an employee's conduct. When someone is fired, not only is his or her income immediately cut off but the person's reputation is also damaged. It may affect their ability to get another job with a comparable salary, and it could also impact family relationships.

This is just one example of issues that develop at work and require wise leadership. Maybe you have had ethics training, or your company makes those decisions from a central office. However, you should be aware of situations that can arise unexpectedly. You may be required to speak up about a coworker's unethical conduct or a tough decision that you are facing:

- A coworker who doesn't keep up with the workload
- A colleague who spreads harmful rumors
- Employees who frequently bicker during the workday
- A manager who favors one employee over the others.

As you reflect on your ethical responsibilities in the organization, you must decide when to intervene and how. Most companies have policies for managing ethical complaints, but others don't. If the business you work for distributes an ethics handbook, become familiar with it and keep it handy for quick reference when needed. Suppose the company doesn't provide ethics training and guidelines for reporting unethical conduct or to help employees follow appropriate protocols. In that case, you can suggest that helpful policies be developed and implemented so that everyone knows how to avoid ethical dilemmas.

Practice Consistent Integrity

Are you the same person at work as you are at home in practicing integrity?

Many of us admit that we are better in one place than the other – sometimes at least. We don't want to lie to loved ones, but we might tell a "little white lie" about the reason for calling off work, claiming a dental appointment instead of a birthday celebration, for example. You might be tempted to take home a handful of pens from the office, but can that be labeled as "stealing"? Answer: Yes.

Antics like these may seem minimal and harmless. But small steps can lead to big problems. An effective leader not only knows what integrity means but also consistently practices it by following the rules and expecting others to do so.

What does it mean to apply integrity on the job? Although duties vary from one employee to another, we all make decisions about the best and right way to do our work. Those decisions involve ethical considerations that determine whether integrity is part of the equation.

Hallie Crawford's article, "How to Achieve Integrity in the Workplace," discusses the importance of integrity when working remotely at home as well as in the public eye:

> So why is it so important to show integrity in the workplace, even when your home is your makeshift office? Here are a few basic reasons:
>
> - Build and maintain a positive reputation

- Earn your boss' trust
- Feel good sticking to your values.[24]

The premise of this book is to prepare you for that shining opportunity of leadership that can develop unexpectedly or after a period of waiting. You will want to be ready to lead others with integrity by demonstrating a positive reputation, trustworthiness, and personal ethics.

Temptation is everywhere. Whether you are reworking the numbers on your travel expense report for more reimbursement or taking home a ream of copy paper, you may think that no one knows or cares. But you know what happened, and someone else might not approve. Don't put yourself under the yoke of guilt and suspicion by doing something that is unnecessary and in violation of company rules.

If you aren't supposed to date coworkers, don't start a flirtation. If you are expected to work an occasional weekend, adjust your personal schedule. If you are taking shortcuts in your work, stop doing it and apologize.

Integrity doesn't mean that you are perfect. It means you continually try to do your best, admit mistakes when they happen, and be open to criticism or suggestions. Ethical conduct is not a quality that can be practiced on occasion. It is a virtue you should embrace daily to build your reputation and contribute to a positive and productive workplace environment.

Maintain Professionalism

One of the chief ways of establishing integrity is to maintain professionalism – the professional conduct expected in the workplace and in your specific role. Here is a definition from Resume.com:

Professionalism is how you display your behavior, attitude and level of skills in the workplace. Being professional at work can be described in many ways, with one of the most agreed-upon definitions being a person's ability to demonstrate a conscientious, courteous and business-oriented manner while on the job. Professionalism is typically always expected within the workplace and is a quality that all employees should strive to embrace and exhibit.[25]

Professionalism promotes courteous conduct and mutual respect. It establishes and enforces workplace boundaries amongst employees, with one another, and with customers or clients. Aspects of professionalism are numerous, and each organization emphasizes those of primary importance.
Examples:

- Compliance – following the rules versus doing things your way
- Diligence – working on schedule versus wasting time
- Accuracy – attention to detail versus careless errors
- Appearance – groomed in business apparel versus scruffiness in casual clothes
- Courtesy – being responsible and polite versus blaming others and behaving rudely.

Some of these, like accuracy and compliance, overlap with ethical practices. Overall, your attitude, behavior, and appearance define who you are and how others will relate to you. Good leaders consider the needs and interests of others. Since leaders are necessarily more visible than other employees in the workplace, they are responsible for establishing integrity and treating others fairly by setting an upright example.

We can define professionalism by what it is not as well as what it is. Everyone recognizes professional individuals by how they speak, dress, and act. Unprofessionalism can be identified in the same way. Specifically, a professional demonstrates self-care as well as concern for others. Respect is the hallmark of that person's conduct. Even during disciplinary actions that must be taken, the professional handles difficult communication with sensitivity to the other individual without demeaning that person. Profanity, yelling, and a dismissive attitude are neither used nor condoned. Emotions are kept in check, except for a hint of kindness, if appropriate.

Indeed.com is a global job resource that provides employment leads and workplace advice. In 2021, the editorial team published a "Guide to Professionalism in the Workplace" that lists ten qualities of job professionalism:

- Reliability
- Humility
- Etiquette
- Neatness
- Consideration
- Dedication
- Organization
- Accountability
- Integrity
- Expertise.[26]

Humility might sound like an odd fit with professionalism. Why? Because we expect high-ranking leaders with valuable expertise to be assertive, if not aggressive, and humility is often misinterpreted as weakness. But the best definition I've heard for humility was stated by a national leader who described it as "power under control." Wow! Harnessing expertise and knowledge to the characteristic of humility equips you with the perfect tools to influence others in encouraging rather than controlling ways.

Etiquette is also a surprising addition to the ten qualities on the list. Good manners are welcome everywhere, but to what extent are they necessary for professionalism in the business world? Indeed.com describes how to demonstrate proper business etiquette in the workplace:

- Greeting new people with a handshake
- Dressing appropriately
- Using professional language and full sentences in written communication
- Putting your phone away during meetings and in face-to-face conversations
- Greeting others by name
- Making eye contact when speaking to others
- Keeping conversation focused on work and avoiding personal topics.

Also included in etiquette are behaviors that are hard to narrowly define and may differ from one organization to the next. For example, companies often have their own dress code that might differ from those of other organizations (more below on this topic). Social media encourages members to use slang and abbreviations as well as skip conventional punctuation, which is acceptable in casual work environments. If your employer does not have etiquette guidelines, why not suggest that guidelines be developed and distributed to all employees, especially new hires?

I have known leaders who did not care much for professionalism. In fact, I remember one or two who thought it "cool" to play by their own rules on the job. Their esoteric manner of dress and offbeat communication style drew the attention they were obviously seeking – but not always in an effective way. People tend to feel more secure in a business-level work environment where professionalism is the norm. When they must deal with mavericks or rebels, it can interfere with job performance.

Leaders may compromise their professionalism and lose the trust of employees and colleagues when they do things like the following:

- Drink too much at lunchtime (versus drink lightly or not at all)
- Socialize with favored employees after hours (versus avoid favorites and treat everyone the same)
- Lock themselves in their office to have a meltdown (versus self-control and honest discussions)
- Yell and scream profanity when employees make honest mistakes (versus a calm manner and objective observations with resulting guidance or discipline, if needed)
- Slam doors and ignore colleagues when angry (versus taking timeouts and then meeting)
- Go missing for hours and are frequently absent (versus using work time ethically).

At your job, even if you don't have a written code of professional guidelines to follow, you can put a promising idea of professionalism into practice by watching those you admire. In fact, a popular tip for climbing the career ladder is to emulate those who are a step or two ahead of you in the job chain: dress, talk, and communicate the way they do.

Other qualities on Indeed's list are common expectations for all employees. To be neat, considerate, resolute, and accountable is the gold standard of conventional integrity. As you contemplate which of these you can incorporate to improve your professional image, the next step is to consider how to represent your employer. You should set your personal interests aside in your role as an organization's leader. There may be overlap between personal and professional interests, but when they are at cross-purposes, the organization's needs must prevail while at work. If that is difficult to conduct, leadership might not be a satisfying career path for you.

Representing the Organization

When adopting leadership qualities from role models to enhance your skills, keep in mind how you plan to represent your company when you accept a leadership role. Managing a department gives you direct oversight of the employees under your supervision. But the higher you go in the organization, the more visible you become – not just to the other employees but also to the public at large – customers, business leaders, and community pillars. Your approach to integrity requires you to present an image that accurately and professionally represents your workplace, whether on the job or after hours. When off the workplace clock, you are free to do as you please. But remember that your company will be judged by how you look and act, even during non-working hours.

You may find it challenging to preserve your way of doing things as you learn how to serve the company's interests. Companies do not, or should not, expect you to breach your personal code of ethics, but they do have expectations for how you represent the business when interacting with coworkers, clients, or the public. This is particularly relevant when connecting with people from other cultures to avoid an unintended gaffe. Cultural sensitivity is another important attribute stemming from integrity.

Dress code is an area that may raise questions. A professional appearance, as indicated above, is the norm in most organizations. But there are degrees of professionalism that vary from casual to formal. You might be used to wearing polo shirts to work, but when preparing for leadership, you may be expected to wear a button-down shirt with a tie – and maybe a jacket. Although three-piece suits are no longer standard office wear, managers often dress in a shirt and tie, especially for special events. But more casual wear, such as miniskirts, body-baring outfits, and extreme colors or patterns, might not be welcome. As you plan for eventual leadership, keep in mind that you will need to dress the part. If you are used to wearing jeans and a pullover, be prepared to update your wardrobe.

Grooming also plays a role when you become a company leader. Facial hair is usually acceptable but find out before growing a six-inch beard. Traditional companies may prefer men not to wear long hair over their ears or collar or halfway down their backs. But norms are changing, and men may be permitted to wear their hair however they wish if it is neat and clean. This is likewise true for employees of different ethnicities or races who might choose to wear hairstyles that reflect their cultural origins or associations. Clean fingernails are a given unless you work in a factory, where your hands are constantly exposed to discoloring substances. Cosmetics, hair color, and clothing trends may be non-negotiable, depending on where you work. Find out if there is a dress code and be ready to follow it.

Political views are another sticking point for leaders. Many want to express their opinions during presentations or in public discussions. But leaders, as well as employees, are expected to keep their views to themselves when they represent the company. However, you may work for an organization that doesn't mind if your views become known. Ask beforehand to avoid potential issues afterward if someone complains.

The same holds true for religious values. You might feel that people will respect you more if they know you have religious scruples. But those beliefs are best kept to yourself at work. Your employer will excuse your absence for your religious holidays. Never assume that is the case, however. Ask ahead of time. The "separation of church and state" principle from the US Constitution has been interpreted by commerce, not just government, in various ways. Your employer may not want you to disclose your religious views and certainly not proselytize colleagues or customers. You might not be permitted to wear religious jewelry or place religious artwork in your workspace. Always check with management if you're unsure.

When asked to represent the company at a community meeting or in client negotiations, be sure you know the expectations of being there, along with boundaries for sharing information or making decisions. Seek clarity in advance to avoid making a mistake.

Personal versus Professional Values

As mentioned above, employees who hope to become leaders need to develop a reputation for integrity. One suggestion is to be the same person at work as at home. But that assumes that you manage your personal life with the same level of integrity as you do at work – with honesty, clarity, and fairness. This also assumes that your home life is built on a foundation of integrity whether you live alone, are married with children, or provide care for an elderly relative.

Horror stories abound of people who seem perfectly respectable on the job and are even viewed as community leaders – but were eventually revealed to be criminals who had committed terrible deeds. These worst-case scenarios are, thankfully, uncommon, but they provide an extreme example of living two lives. Employees who live double lives demanding considerable time and effort cannot be fully committed to either. Lapses will occur, and people on both sides will become frustrated or disappointed. Avoid disreputable behaviors that could land you in legal trouble and put the company in a bad light.

An employee, Ben, tried to juggle being a househusband of four children with a full-time professional position. Ben managed to stay calm and competently oversee most job duties, but he often missed meetings to pick up kids or take them to medical appointments. He also was not the first person to volunteer for new assignments. His balancing act was noticed by colleagues who collectively commented to the supervisor conducting Ben's annual performance review. The supervisor explained to Ben that his job performance had dropped and suggested ways of helping him manage family responsibilities, such as carpooling and hiring a caregiver for afterschool hours so Ben could attend staff meetings. He accepted some of these suggestions, and his performance improved, but the stigma label of "shirker" never quite disappeared.

Another associate building his career took a second job utilizing his creative talents. Like Ben, Sam missed occasional meetings and failed to step up to important company initiatives. Called on the carpet for increased absenteeism, Sam agreed to give less time to the second job and put more time into his primary position. Eventually, as he re-established his integrity, he was promoted to a leadership role.

Some companies don't care what you do in your personal

life: train for a marathon, raise a prize-winning garden or work a part-time second job. Other companies require you to report outside activities that involve considerable amounts of time or income to avoid a conflict of interest. If your company has this policy, honestly report any activities that might raise concerns. It's better to reveal this information up front and be told how to manage the situation directly rather than have someone report you and lead others to think you tried to conceal your external activities.

On the other hand, domestic issues are best kept private. Of course, if you and your spouse welcome a new child to the family, you will probably make a proud but informal announcement to your coworkers. But if your marriage is going through a rocky phase, you should not discuss it openly at work. You might have a close friend to confide in, but you should not share personal matters with everyone. A tragic event like a family member's death or divorce can be discreetly mentioned to the people affected by your absenteeism at work as you deal with personal issues. But avoid spilling your family secrets at work to everyone in your department, which could raise questions about your professionalism.

Integrity is a vital part of who you are personally and on the job. It is a valuable building block for your professional reputation and leadership potential. Avoid missteps that can take you in the wrong direction and damage your integrity for years to come. The rumor mill is constantly working to exploit minor issues into full-blown crises that can torpedo your leadership journey. Maintain your integrity even when things go wrong to continue establishing a reputation of reliability and trust.

Chapter 7

Communicate Effectively

Are you a good communicator? Would others agree?

I heard about a supervisor who managed a company of about 80 employees. Smart and visionary, he was liked by most and demonstrated effective leadership. Just one thing about Joe bothered people: He didn't maintain prompt or clear communication. It was because he was so busy and determined to oversee numerous operations simultaneously. But many noticed that he did not respond to e-mails promptly and sometimes not at all. Some of these messages had a timeline attached: His employees needed approvals for proposals that could save the company money, or his authorization was required for staff to attend a professional conference. They tried to catch him in the halls or after a meeting. Other times they would schedule brief appointments to get the necessary information.

Busy executives often deal with pressure to prioritize tasks and keep up with the communication flow. Most of Joe's employees were patient as they waited to hear from their leader, and sometimes they would contact his administrative assistant for help. But there were near misses on important deadlines. Overall, Joe did an excellent job and was admired for his ability to keep things running smoothly.

But his employees wished he would be more conscientious about responding to e-mails and questions that would facilitate their day-to-day work.

Communication is an essential skill every leader needs. Studies show that managers and supervisors spend as much as 80 percent of the workday reading as well as communicating via writing or speaking. The ability to interact effectively and clearly in a timely manner with colleagues and coworkers is an asset that benefits everyone.

A few years ago, I heard about two candidates being considered for a job promotion in a county engineering department. One had more job experience, and the other had taken additional college writing classes. The department hired the applicant who had taken additional writing classes as they felt that skill would be a positive in working with other department employees as well as the public.

Leadership Choice, a leadership training program, outlines four key benefits of effective communication at work:

1. Conflict mitigation
2. Employee engagement
3. Better client relationships
4. Productive and talented workforce.[27]

Let's explore these four benefits and how they can be established in our leadership through effective communication.

Preventing Conflict

One wrong word or response or no response can trigger a colleague into venting frustration and anger. Let's say an employee in your department is working on a team project, but the other employees are not doing their share of work on the project. When you are informed of the problem, the hardworking employee will expect you to do something about it. But if you're silent or noncommittal, that employee may feel insignificant or even betrayed.

A leader's role is to mediate conflicts and help employees find a solution that works for everyone. The way in which you respond or don't will serve as a measure for employees to determine your leadership skill. So it's not just the words you use or the psychological strategies you apply that represent communication style. People will also notice your timeliness and attention to issues.

An initiative-taking approach to monitoring systems for which a leader is responsible can head off problems before they cause serious trouble. Checklists, inspections, and reviews identify issues and enable a leader to address them to prevent employee frustration that may lead to conflict.

Employee Interactions

Are you an open-door communicator? You may have heard the expression "The door is always open" by those who want to be transparent and accessible at work. If you frequently rush from place to place and barely notice employees as you rush by, your actions convey the idea that those employees are unimportant. But if your office door is truly open, literally and figuratively, then your organization knows that you welcome questions, concerns, and requests for assistance from anyone at almost any time. When employees feel like they matter to management, they work better and harder. But it is up to you to maintain clear and consistent communication so they can speak their mind and get the help they need.

Staying connected with employees can head off problems that might otherwise fester. As discussed in chapter 6, it's important to stay calm, listen carefully, and clarify key points. Impartiality is essential. When someone brings a complaint or concern to you, be prepared to listen objectively and respond clearly. Employees deserve to be heard and understood.

Later in this chapter, I will explain how to deliver bad news in a way that mitigates a complainant's resentment and irritation.

Client Relationships

Maintaining positive relationships with customers and clients is critical to succeeding in a business. Companies often have a schedule or calendar to coordinate routine contact with customers, like sending automated greeting cards for birthdays, anniversaries or holidays. But like employees, clients like to feel appreciated. Using the body language tips covered in chapter 6 can help convey this: eye contact, bodily stance, and voice intonation.

Prompt and precise communication is vital. Have you ever tried scheduling a service visit from a professional, and nobody called you back after you left a message? How did you feel when you had to call two or three times to talk to someone and finally get an appointment?

Your clients feel the same way when they cannot reach you, or leave a message that you don't respond to right away. Yes, you are busy, but so are they. Experts claim it is cheaper to maintain current customers than to solicit new ones. Establish solid relationships with your clients by responding promptly to their calls and messages. If you don't have the information they need, explain that you will get back to them as soon as possible. You can also have your assistant or secretary respond to their calls with the requested information.

Productivity

Have you ever participated in a relay race where each team member must dash a distance with an object and hand it to the next team member? Each one does the same thing until everyone has taken a lap. Two or more teams compete to determine which team can complete the relay first.

On a larger scale, the relay system operates in many companies in an analogous way. Each employee can only do their part when the people ahead and behind them do their parts. The team leader coaches everyone to act quickly and correctly according to the rules. To quote an old saying, "A chain is only as strong as its weakest link." The relay team is only as successful as its slowest member. Your company is only as productive as its weakest operations point.

It's up to the leader to monitor the process and ensure everyone is doing their part without hindrance. Leaders need to provide guidance and troubleshoot problems that arise to keep all systems operating efficiently. Communication plays a key role in getting things done quickly and accurately. If an employee must stand around waiting for approval to order a repair part or confirmation to proceed with the scheduled initiative, valuable time is lost. As they say in the business world, time is money, so weak or nonexistent communication costs the organization profit and employee goodwill.

Keep Accurate Records

Maintaining complete, up-to-date records on interactions and transactions is another cardinal quality for leadership. Although it is the support staff's responsibility to coordinate major databases and files, the leader must ensure that documentation is preserved for every facet of operations. Copies of invoices, memos, reports, and contracts are amongst the most common documents kept on file. But you should document anything more than a casual exchange with customers or employees for the following reasons:

- **Confirmation.** When people discuss a topic, it is easy for details to get lost or forgotten. A written record can straighten things out if the topic later becomes a point of contention. Leaders or leaders in training may want to keep a daily log of meaningful interactions, even if some seem insignificant at the time. Specific forms can be used to document appointment activities, such as interviewing a job applicant. If the applicant later claims a certain salary was offered during the interview, for example, the written record can document whether that is accurate.

- **Backup.** In a busy department, it's not unusual for a document to be misplaced or lost. Someone takes an order by phone and forgets an important detail. Keep a folder online or in your office for records of transactions or interactions in case the primary document cannot be located. The person in charge or responsible for various aspects of the organization should know who maintains the official file and how to request access when needed.

- **Legality.** If a conflict evolves into a legal claim, the court will require copies of pertinent documents as evidence for the case. Without documentation as proof, the claim is weakened. Receipts, e-mails, and even social media posts have been used in litigation to support a plaintiff's or defendant's case. An administrator's log of daily events in the office clarifies the uncertainty of if, for example, an expected delivery arrived that day. Although an official record can confirm the delivery's arrival, the record could be misfiled or inaccurately completed.

Managers don't need to track every office activity, however, as the notated files would become too cumbersome to manage. Here are sample communications that could be added to a leader's daily log:

- Telephone discussion notes
- Meeting summaries
- Client interactions
- Customer complaints
- Employee conflicts
- Employees who go above and beyond
- News that affects the company
- Suggestions for improvement.

Listing noteworthy events will provide a helpful point of reference if needed. In my experience, that has happened on several occasions.

Since you may not have time to deal with everything on your list each day, adding a date and a few summary points will serve as a placeholder until you have time to deal with them.

Maintain Confidentiality

The universal need for confidentiality should be obvious, but it might be worth emphasizing here in case you let your guard down. We touched on the topic of confidentiality in the last chapter but let me emphasize it more here with respect to communication.

We live in an age of heightened security. Have you tried counting the security devices you pass on your way to work, school, business, or shopping? Surveillance cameras monitor our movements, from neighbors' home security systems to parking lot monitoring systems, streetlight or lamppost cameras, indoor and outdoor video recordings, and in public buildings. Despite our collective loss of privacy, we must do our best to protect the privacy of those within our sphere of influence.

When a creditor, attorney, or prospective employer contacts you for information about a current employee, be careful about what you say. The only information you can rightfully share is whatever the employee authorizes you to divulge. Laws may vary depending on where you are doing business, but you might not be able even to confirm whether a person is or has been an employee. Even if you can legally confirm that fact, it might not be possible for you to reveal when the person was hired, the job title, or the salary. Make sure you check relevant employment laws in your area before speaking to someone about an employee. An exception to this principle is if law enforcement agencies contact you about a legal matter. Again, find out from applicable laws how much you can say about a current or past employee.

The same policy applies to documentation. Don't share an employee's documents with anyone, even a family member, until you can confirm your legal right to do so. In some places, an employee must sign a release form permitting you to share specific information with certain entities. If you are asked about an employee from a public entity, check with that person before revealing job-related or personal information.

Government agencies, like an unemployment bureau, might require details about an employee's job duties if that person applies for unemployment benefits after leaving your company. You may be asked to complete an agency form to verify the person's former employment. Another possibility is that an employee who works for your company or one who is no longer employed could request a job reference. The general rule is to ask the employee what information you are allowed to share and with whom.

Be careful about discussing one employee with another, even in a casual manner. If the talked-about employee finds out, you might face a legal claim of defamation or a related charge, even if that was not your intent. Information is a valuable commodity that should be managed carefully.

Good News

Good news! Announcing good news at work is easy and welcomed by recipients. A positive news message is not difficult to craft, and you will enjoy making others happy. Common reasons to write a good-news message in a letter, e-mail, or other format include events like approving vacation leave, offering a pay raise, or granting a job promotion. The same format can be used for simple messages or information updates.

1. State the good news in the first paragraph (about two or three sentences): "Your request for conference funding is approved…"

2. Explain the details in the second paragraph (about three or four sentences): "Please submit your conference expenses by the end of the month to the business office, and reimbursement will be deposited within five days."

3. Finalize or recap the good news in the last paragraph

(about two or three sentences): "We look forward to hearing your conference report at next month's staff meeting. Thank you for representing our company at this important industry event."

This is a basic example. Paragraph length can vary. You may need additional paragraphs to explain a more complex situation, such as approving overseas travel for a business trip.

Neutral information updates can be organized the same way, and in certain cases, you will not need to write as much.

1. State the facts in the first paragraph: "The first-floor men's restroom will be closed for repairs the rest of this week."

2. Explain the details: "Please use the second-floor level restroom until next Monday."

3. Close with a call for questions: "E-mail the maintenance manager if you have questions."

All three parts of this brief message could be compressed into one paragraph but separating the message into three topic parts will help readers not to overlook any details.

Bad News

If you've ever had to send a negative message, you probably didn't enjoy it. Not only do we dislike looking like the bad guy, but we also don't like making anyone feel bad. Sometimes it's unavoidable. An employee makes a mistake. Someone gets hurt. A promotion is denied. The budget is too tight for a raise. These and countless other disappointments are processed every day in the workplace.

Keep in mind that unwelcome news is anything that diverts the recipient's attention from their work, unless it involves good news. Asking someone to explain a procedure, listen to your idea, give you time off, or even make a presentation, which puts the speaker in a favorable light with the audience, can be viewed as a negative task to address. Look for ways to make an unpleasant or unwelcome request palatable to the other person.

- Can I take you to lunch to get your thoughts on a new customer service idea?

- I can spend a few hours this weekend helping your department catch up in return for you giving my staff a demonstration of the new product being rolled out.

- The local business chamber would love to hear about your legendary expertise with the company and can offer you a free membership or a $100 stipend.

Asking someone to do something is tricky. The person might lack the time or interest in helping. Similarly, delivering bad news is difficult. But it must be done, and a leader is expected to convey difficult information to the people being impacted. Here is a recommended format:

1. In paragraph one, begin on a positive or neutral note (three or four sentences): "The company has just received a sizable order from a new client that must be filled immediately. If we do an excellent job, the client promises to place ongoing orders with us."

2. In paragraph two, include details that lead up to the "bad news" (three or four sentences): "We will make this a priority order ahead of existing orders that can wait a few days. We expect it will take about two weeks to fill, check, and ship the new order."

3. In paragraph three, state the bad news clearly and succinctly (three or four sentences): "To meet the customer's shipping need, lunchtime will temporarily be reduced from 60 to 30 minutes. You will be financially compensated for a 45-minute lunch break. If everything goes smoothly, the full lunch hour will be reinstated when the order has shipped."

4. Close with a positive or encouraging statement (two or three sentences): "Thank you for being hardworking employees. Because of you, our company has this opportunity to attract new customers. With consistent effort, we hope to provide attractive bonuses at the end of the fiscal year."

Of course, some readers prefer to see the bad news in the first paragraph instead of waiting until later in the communication. But by providing a rationale that leads up to the bad news, readers are less likely to get frustrated or disappointed and more apt to understand the reasons for the unwelcome news. Thus, you may get a more positive response.

Communication Tips

A good leader chooses words carefully as they can wound or heal. Some situations call for fewer words and a simple approach. Others require detailed rationales or explanations.

After drafting your message, review it for stylistic effects like those below. When organizing written messages and presentations, the following tips can help you produce clear, uncluttered communication.

- Avoid overusing "I" or any form of first person. You will sometimes have to refer to yourself to explain an experience or a situation, but when possible, keep the focus on the event or object. Explaining more about what happened than about your role in it. Example: "I have news you will enjoy about this year's vacation policy." Improved: "You are going to enjoy this vacation policy update."

- Keep the focus on the audience by using second-person pronouns: "You have become a genuine asset to this company through innovation and reliability."

- When you must use "I," avoid starting several sentences with it. Example: "I am here today to explain the new procedures handbook." Improved: "The new procedures handbook will be explained in this meeting."

- End sentences with a strong word (noun) rather than a weak one (preposition). Example: "You have given this department a reputation to be proud of." Improved: "You have given our department pride in our reputation."

- Avoid using negative terms for unwelcome news; use positive ones when feasible. Example: "The customer's order will arrive a week after its November 20 due date." Improved: "The customer's order will arrive no later than December 1."

- Use clear descriptors, concrete nouns, and action verbs. Example: "She is a funny person." (is "funny" meaning humorous or odd?) Improved: "She displays a keen sense of humor." Example: "He shows a lot of patience." Improved: "He doesn't complain when job duties are shifted."

- Avoid overusing "to be" and "to have" (intransitive) verbs. Example: "We will be having a great dinner at customer appreciation night." Improved: "We will be dining on prime rib and roast chicken at customer appreciation night."

- Avoid redundancy and repetition. Example: "The meeting agenda will circle back to last month's topic of pay raises." Improved: "The meeting agenda will return to last month's topic of pay raises."

You might think some of these "rules" are unnecessary. Maybe. But a thoughtful communicator plans each message by considering audience needs and perspectives. We often compose a speech or memo as a means of self-expression. A careful read-through will help find ways of making your words more meaningful to your audience. Remember the adage "The pen is mightier than the sword"? You don't need a sword to run a company, but well-placed words can make a massive impact in motivating, guiding, and supporting employees and customers.

Chapter 8

Continue to Grow

A long-time friend shared a story about someone who influenced his career. Jim, not his real name, and I met to catch up and discuss our career journeys, and Jim told me he had almost quit his first professional job in marketing when dealing with an overly critical boss. He felt "Mr. D" highlighted too many tiny details for correction and ignored Jim's creativity and work ethic.

"What made you stay?" I asked.

"My colleague Jocelyn," he answered. "She was in another department but used to work for the same boss. Bringing around some forms for Mr. D's signature, Jocelyn witnessed a tense critique from Mr. D of my work, and she invited me to lunch at the company cafeteria. I assumed it was to share some warnings to help me avoid getting fired. As we ate, Jocelyn offered insight from her experience in that department.

"Don't take him too seriously," she said. "Some employers love to see creativity, but not in this case. Mr. D blows a lot of steam because he prefers the old way of doing things, and he is testing your mettle to see if you're up for the job. Just make sure you manage projects the way he likes them, and he'll go easier on you. There will be opportunities to exercise your creativity and try new ways of doing things later."

"Sure enough," Jim said, "when Mr. D noticed I was following his guidance without suggesting alternative methods, he relaxed. I even saw him smile." We chuckled. Jim continued, "We got along pretty well after that, and I stayed with the company a few more years until I got a higher-level position elsewhere based on experience shaped in part by Mr. D's influence."

"So," I asked, "Jocelyn influenced your attitude toward Mr. D?"

"Yes – and I've learned to ask for advice from seasoned employees like her who have experienced the type of issues with which I'm struggling. Everyone should have a mentor while building their careers and throughout their work life."

Recruit a Mentor

The Indeed.com article, "24 Reasons Why Mentorship Is Important," shows the continuing popularity and success of mentorship in the workplace. What exactly is a mentor, and how do you find one?

> A mentor is someone who acts as an advisor to a less experienced individual, known as their mentee. Typically, individuals seek mentors who work in their same or desired field. The mentor helps this individual grow and develop as a professional, often offering advice based on their more advanced knowledge or experience. Mentorship relationships can be built through networking, personal connections, or formal mentorship programs.[28]

If you've had or currently have a career mentor, you probably agree the benefits are mutual and valuable in building your career. Some people meet with their mentor routinely while playing golf or over breakfast, for example. Others have a more casual approach by meeting occasionally or when a question arises that an experienced mentor might be able to answer.

You can have more than one mentor or switch mentors over time as your career trajectory advances. Here are suggestions for finding a mentor with whom you can build a professional relationship:

- Reach out to a higher-ranking or more experienced colleague at your job.

- Join a community civic group like the Kiwanis or Rotary and connect with someone in your job field.

- Become a member of the local chamber of commerce, attend events, and find a person who may be willing to advise you in work-related matters.

- Participate in professional groups or organizations where you may meet someone with similar work experience or background (church, volunteerism, charity boards).

You may need to casually "interview" prospective mentors to see if they have the time, interest, and job experience you require. It could take time, but the effort is worthwhile for many mentees.

Benefits of having a mentor are numerous, as suggested in the above article and others. You might develop greater insight into accountability, goal setting, applicable knowledge, and professional growth. You may someday want to mentor other new employees. For now, a mentor can help you navigate the challenges of your work life.

Not all mentors are the same. You may want to work with someone who has tackled the problems of your occupation, such as environmental law compliance or mastering the next iteration of a technology application. Another type of mentor can help you prepare for leadership roles by focusing on the topics addressed in this book. Some mentoring relationships may be short-term. Others could last a lifetime.

A thoughtful mentor offers more than occasional advice or a helping hand. They often point you to resources that have helped their career journey or have recently become available. Workshops, training, certifications, books, videos, and organizations are some of the tools that mentors can suggest in addition to their personal experience and insight.

If your company does not currently sponsor a mentoring program by pairing seasoned employees with new hires, you might suggest that one be implemented. Training for mentors can be as simple as tapping a long-time employee to share expertise with newbies and answer questions as needed. Professional mentoring programs are available in workshops or training programs to ensure a productive process develops at a participating worksite.

When selecting a mentor, keep in mind that the person is donating time and experience to help you build a successful career. To make the relationship work efficiently, you can do the following:

- Let your mentor know upfront about problems or questions you would like to address.
- Explain your availability and ask about your mentor's schedule, e.g., Saturday mornings.
- Indicate your preferred contact mode – phone, text message, or e-mail – and ask the mentor's preference.
- Decide whether meetings will be routine or spontaneous.

You can prepare to collaborate with a mentor by doing the following:

- Arrive on time and don't overstay the visit, except by mutual agreement.

- Be prepared to share your ideas and concerns succinctly and briefly.

- Keep an open mind to your mentor's advice – you don't have to accept everything, but politely hear what the person has to say.

- Express thanks for the mentor's investment of time on your behalf. This could occasionally take the form of an appreciative greeting card or buying a meal.

- If things don't work out as expected, be courteous in ending the relationship or changing the arrangement: "I appreciate your help and will be in touch the next time something comes up."

In some cases, having a mentor, especially one who is trained for the role or has been assigned by the company, can be listed in your resume to show your willingness to go the extra mile in learning your job and building a professional future. Mentors often add value to your job experience and your career journey.

Join an Accountability Group

All employees are expected to be responsible and accountable for the outcomes of their work. In other words, if they design a product that doesn't turn a profit, they will need to redesign that product. But if the designer passes blame to the sales force or the marketing team, that product's success might be doomed to failure.

Marlo Oster, in "How to Build a Culture of Accountability in the Workplace," explains the concept:

> Accountability in the workplace means the buck stops with you. It's not just about completing the tasks that are assigned to you; it's owning the end result.
>
> To be held accountable often has a negative connotation. In fact, if you search synonyms for *accountable*, "punishable" is chief on the list. While it's an element of being accountable, fear of punishment does not contribute to a healthy work environment.
>
> Being accountable at work means your team can rely on you to own your mistakes and your successes, to never shift the blame to someone else or shirk your duties, and to always meet the expectations set by your organization.[29]

You learned accountability as a child by caring for a pet or supervising a younger sibling. In college, you might have had a study partner with whom you shared accountability for completing a joint project. If so, you understand the importance of not only completing an expected action but also being responsible for the outcome.

For example, if you overfeed your puppy and it becomes sick, you should accept the responsibility and be more careful when feeding the pet. Family members might notice the puppy's illness and investigate the problem by questioning you to determine what happened and implement a corrective course of action. If the family ignored the problem or decided to let someone else feed the puppy without helping you understand you did wrong, similar problems or a careless attitude will continue unchecked.

Matt McLaughlin at elustraconsulting.com emphasizes the valuable benefits that come from working with an accountability group:

> Accountability is a major influence in attaining your goals. The American Society of Training and Development studied accountability and found that people are 65% more likely to reach their goals when they've shared them with someone else. Even better, people are 95% more likely to reach their goals when they share them with a group and meet regularly to review them.
>
> Although some employees prefer working alone, an accountability group brings people together to share job goals, manage challenges, address problems, and celebrate successes. This team approach enables groups to productively reach individual or team goals.[30]

Like mentoring, an accountability group can be as simple as several employees meeting now and then for coffee and a progress report on current projects. Members can offer feedback or suggest ideas to each person's raised issues. More than that, they can help one another take ownership of their work and perform it to the best of their ability. They encourage one another to remember that the outcomes of each person's efforts impact the work lives of many. In the workplace hierarchy, one person's effort, or lack of it because of inadequate training or slacking off, has a direct bearing on other employees within a department, a division, or company. Outcomes also impact customers and sometimes the public at large.

When organizing or joining an accountability group, keep the following in mind:

- **Work with a well-rounded group of employees who can help one another in their respective ways.** For example, someone from the accounting department can review a project budget and give an opinion on its feasibility. A marketing division employee might highlight features of a new product that could be enhanced to attract consumer interest. Everyone is held accountable to complete a successful project, product, or initiative before presenting it to the higher-ups for approval.

- **Take accountability seriously.** This should not be a group that meets only to satisfy an administrator's request or boost members' egos. Everyone should be committed. It may help to take notes. Honest feedback is paramount. Criticism should be given and received graciously.

- **Follow up with previous concerns, complaints, or suggestions.** At the next meeting, explain what you've done to address accountability issues that were previously outlined.

- **Look for patterns of improvement.** If the same issues keep coming up, make changes for better outcomes. Consider the group as an opportunity for growth and development.

- **Maintain professionalism.** Always be polite and listen carefully to what is said, even when you don't agree. Remember that everyone is volunteering their time to come together as a group for the betterment of all.

- **Make adjustments.** If the group is not working well together, bow out politely and form or find another accountability group. Don't gossip about what was said or done by the others. Stay focused on how you can benefit from a well-organized accountability group.

Teamwork can be inspiring when everyone collaborates as a cohesive unit despite their differences. Do your part to contribute meaningful feedback and accept sincere suggestions on how to become an even more valuable employee – and someday a leader.

Get Additional Training

No matter what your current level of education is, it is vital that you continue to grow in your workplace and leadership skills. You won't necessarily need to have a college degree to get a top-level career position, as you can see from this list of successful career-builders and entrepreneurs:

- Bill Gates dropped out of Harvard to pursue technology interests and eventually became one of the richest people in the world after co-founding Microsoft.

- Richard Branson, founder of Virgin Atlantic Airways, dropped out of high school at age 16 after struggling with dyslexia but subsequently became a successful and influential innovator.

- Anne Beiler, co-founder of Auntie Anne's Pretzels, grew up in an Amish community and sold her pretzels at a local farm market. By 2005, after five years and 100 franchise locations, her pretzels earned $250 million, and she sold the business to become a motivational speaker and author.

Even though these individuals did not seek a college degree, they were lifelong learners in the areas of their passion. Many of the world's best-known and wealthiest entrepreneurs are avid readers and have taught themselves valuable skills that have helped advance their careers.

While most people don't necessarily plan to become world-renowned millionaires, many strive to be top-notch in their field. Those who became leaders have typically learned new skills and ways of thinking. Similarly, you may be able to benefit from additional education or training.

Here are simple but highly effective strategies for becoming more knowledgeable in your own right and more valuable to your employer, which may help land you a leader's role.

- **Earn a training certificate.** Companies sometimes offer training courses to help employees update current skills or learn new ones. Sometimes this training is optional, and other times it is required. Company-sponsored training programs may last anywhere from half a day to several weeks. If required, do your best to master the skills being taught.

    Consider participating in optional training to advance your credentials and make yourself a more valuable employee. Not only will the skill be helpful, but the initiative you took to enroll in optional training voluntarily will show your commitment to self-improvement and dedication to enhancing your value to your job and the organization.

    Training certificates, when awarded, make an excellent addition to your personnel file. Be sure your boss receives a copy of the certificate. It can serve as a bargaining chip for job rewards like working from home or a pay increase during the annual performance review. Training provided by the company is free, so take advantage of it when you can.

- **Take accredited college courses.** If you want to study more job-specific subjects or gradually work toward a college degree, register for an occasional college class related to your current job or future career goals. For example, if you work in accounts payable but would like to become a CPA, take a couple of accounting courses to enhance your knowledge. Even a couple of classes might help you better understand and perform in your current position. If the classes go well, you may decide to keep going and earn a degree.

    Many classes are now offered online, so you can study at home when convenient. Financial aid can be plentiful in some instances, so check with the college's financial aid office to see if you are eligible for tuition assistance. Your company might also have a tuition reimbursement benefit that will repay your tuition fees if you pass a job-related course with a grade of C or higher.

- **Earn additional job experience.** If you lack the time or resources to get job training or take college courses, you might want to look into volunteering to gain experience. Perhaps you can spend time on Saturday mornings or one evening per week at a company where you can learn by observing and assisting.

    For example, if you currently work as a home health aide assisting the elderly or chronically ill at home, you may aspire for a higher-level position, such as a nurse practitioner. Consider volunteering in a medical office or hospital where you can assist without being obtrusive. As a form of job shadowing, you can see what the position is like and the skills needed as well as learn the highs and lows of that job. If you later decide to take classes, you will be better prepared and possibly earn college credits for the volunteer hours you have put in.

Occupations like sales, education, and business frequently advertise for volunteers or interns to work without pay or at low pay while earning valuable work experience. If you have time, this is another way to build credibility toward a career position and eventual leadership.

A 2012 article in *The Journal of Leadership Education* titled "Enhancing Leadership Skills in Volunteers" explores the role of volunteerism in shaping one's self-perception of leadership identity within a group:

> **Changing Perceptions of Groups**
> Being an active participant in volunteer groups tends to change individual perceptions of our groups. Volunteers sometimes begin their involvement viewing the volunteer program as just a collection of friends or like-minded people. As they better understand the purposes of the program, this collection of people begins to be seen and understood as an organization with structure and roles. Eventually, volunteers will see the volunteer program as an entity to develop and that they have a leadership responsibility within that group development.[31]

Whatever your lifestyle circumstances, these opportunities can help you develop your leadership potential. You don't have to struggle blindly, feeling incompetent in a new or difficult position. Other employees at your company or elsewhere can help, so don't be afraid to ask.

Since resources like these are free or affordable, take advantage of them to develop your abilities for professional development. You can overcome challenges to build new skills and strengths as you prepare for that shining moment of leadership.

Chapter 9

Get Involved

In the last chapter, we examined simple, effective ways to build your job skills by connecting to professional sources of knowledge, including training and education. We explored the options of mentorship, accountability groups, and volunteering as attainable growth opportunities. These tools are commonplace and often lead to significant returns on your investment of time and effort. In connecting with professionals in your occupation, you can benefit from their expertise, which could help your career grow in leaps and bounds.

Now let's look at additional sources of expertise and networking to develop strategic skills and prepare you for a leadership role. To introduce these options, let me share another story from prior experience.

An author of history and business books was invited through her PR rep to speak at an exclusive book club meeting in an upscale part of town. About 20 members attended and were thrilled to meet this author. During the group's dinner and subsequent book discussion, the writer made such a positive impression on the members that two attendees invited her to speak to their respective groups at upcoming events, which she was happy to do. The author had expected to chat with a handful of readers about her book. Instead, she met two dozen members of the book club, several of whom bought books after her talk, and she was invited to additional events.

This type of chain reaction can happen as you collaborate with community groups who share your interests. When invited to attend a special interest meeting, try to find time to participate, as you may meet like-minded people who can help you grow professionally. They might be able to open doors for your career advancement or assist you in making additional connections. Sometimes you can make significant career progress by getting involved with business organizations interested in your vocation.

Join Business Organizations

At any stage of your career, getting involved with the business community in your area is advisable. Several advantages could materialize from getting acquainted with professionals in your line of work through structured meetings or casual gatherings.

- **Exchange ideas and share stories of struggles or success.** Knowing that others have similar job experiences may help you feel less isolated. You can swap suggestions for coping with stressful situations, such as following a new dress code that seems overreaching or being expected to stay at your desk without breaks, except for a short lunch period. Certain policies may be justified when the rationale is explained by those who have experienced similar situations at their place of employment. If others agree your work policies are unfair, you can together brainstorm ways of crafting an appropriate response.

- **Build camaraderie.** As discussed in the previous chapter, getting to know others in your field might lead to mentoring relationships or group accountability. You can become acquainted organically without having to search broadly for a professional support system. You might also just enjoy getting to know people in your occupation with whom you can "talk shop."

- **Establish valuable connections.** When you meet other businesspeople, you can make associations that lead to new customers or clients, better deals on supplies or equipment, opportunities for promotion and advancement, and the potential for project coordination and collaboration. You might also be able to build bridges between companies for expansive joint projects.

- **Cultivate personal growth and development.** Networking with professionals can open doors to helpful training offered by relevant organizations. They might recommend a workshop or seminar that could strengthen your job skills. You could be invited to give a talk or author an article related to your job that will be published in the organization's newsletter, blog, social media, or website. You gain insight from being around people who have been in the business longer than you.

- **Impress your boss.** Joining professional organizations show you are dedicated to learning new things about your occupation or the industry. Using personal time to attend meetings, give presentations, and hold officer positions contributes to your preparation for leadership. You will be viewed as an ambitious person interested in lead roles for the community or your industry.

- **Observe leadership styles.** When you join community business groups, you can see how the leaders perform and the effect of their leadership style on the group's initiatives or objectives. This will broaden your exposure to other leadership styles and help influence your preferred approach. You will also see how the group members respond to their leaders for ideas about what you should or should not do when your turn comes.

You can join business groups either physically in your city or region or online, where you can attend via Zoom or another videoconferencing app. Meetings are usually scheduled monthly. If you can't participate in all the regular meetings, at least go occasionally to reap the benefits.

Local professional organizations may include Rotary, Lions, or the chamber of commerce. Towns and suburbs sometimes have their own business groups. You can also participate in city council meetings to get acquainted with other professionals. Become a board member of the library, credit union, or another organization you believe in. Even if it is not related to your vocation, you can learn a great deal from being part of a professional group.

Before deciding which groups to join, attend a couple of meetings as a visitor. It may also help to read their newsletter or social media posts for information about their mission and the type of activities they sponsor. Participating in one or two meetings as a visitor will help you decide whether this is an organization you want to be part of.

If you cannot find a professional group of interest, you might want to start one. Look for potential members to recruit amongst coworkers and networking sites, such as LinkedIn or Facebook. Arrange an informal meeting at a centrally located coffee shop for others to learn more about the group and its goals.

Being part of a professional business group can further your self-directed leadership training. Expanding contacts, observing leaders in action, and learning new skills in a group setting could accelerate your leadership progress.

Participate in Community Causes

Whenever I notice local businesses or employees supporting a community issue or sponsoring a fundraiser for an individual struggling with unemployment or health problems, I like to do business with them. If they are caring enough to help those in need, they deserve customer loyalty.

I know supermarkets, for example, that post flyers and set out collection receptacles for children who have cancer. A community bowling alley has been known to donate to and coordinate community gifts for the family of a fallen firefighter killed in the line of duty. I appreciate businesses that aid those in need. By demonstrating leadership in these personal community traumas, they set an example and pave the way for customers to do the same.

Outside of your employee duties, look for ways to give back to the community where you live or work. If you enjoy sports, become a volunteer coach for a Little League team. If coaching requires more time than you can spare, donate to the team. Whatever your personal interests, you can find ways to support the local community through assistance to programs like literacy by tutoring a few hours a week or organizing a cleanup day for a nearby park. Volunteerism of this type can help you expand your leadership skills by learning how such programs are formed and operated. You can also add your volunteer experience and skills to your annual job performance evaluation or future employment applications.

If your schedule permits, participate in activities like a town council, education board meetings, or election day registration. When long-term volunteer commitments feel daunting, you can get involved in occasional volunteer-supported events like a library book sale or a playground renovation project. You may meet like-minded people who might eventually inform you of job openings that would welcome your work experience and community action skills. As you get acquainted with the movers and shakers in your area, you will have more opportunities to donate your talents to causes and organizations that seem most worthwhile. You can also expand your connections more broadly in ways that could one day further your career.

Another benefit of becoming locally involved is that you can develop a skill that could evolve into leadership status. I knew a young woman who volunteered for a social service agency. She was then offered a part-time paid position, which she accepted. A year later, she was invited to apply for a full-time job at that organization, but she decided the time was not right as she still had young children in elementary school. However, two years later, she accepted a full-time paid leadership role training the volunteers. This person's initial experience helping the agency enabled her to build skills and credentials that prepared her to eventually train others based on her experience and insight. Not only that, but the people she worked with also had the opportunity to get acquainted with the young woman. They admired her eagerness to do quality work with a pleasant demeanor. She demonstrated attributes that showed she would make a powerful addition to the company.

Even if your community contributions don't directly lead

to a managerial role, you could share your newfound abilities with others through a personal or industry-related blog or an article for the area newspapers or a trade journal. As you establish an expert identity online or in print, this will be another way of highlighting your leadership abilities.

Use Social Media Responsibly

Social media users have multiplied exponentially in the past few years. Facebook, Instagram, YouTube, and Reddit are a handful of the most popular websites where people go to connect with others, be entertained, or find useful information. Businesses and organizations use social media as well. These platforms offer a convenient, free, and globally accessible medium for advertising and marketing, along with building customer relations. LinkedIn is the premier business media site that attracts jobseekers and career-builders who connect with companies and services where they can find suitable employment.

If you are assigned the company role of selecting which social media platforms to use, decide which will best reach your customers since each tailors its content to specific user interests, as Gary Henderson suggests in his article, "How To Use Social Media For Business":

> Marketing is all about reaching people in the right place with the right message at the right time, and if you get your choice of platform wrong, you can end up reaching the wrong people in the wrong place at the wrong time.
>
> Spend time revisiting your buyer personas (if you have them) and figuring out which social media channels they're likely to be active on.

Then work out why they're there.

If you provide executive coaching, for example, then your audience might be using Facebook to keep up with their family, Twitter to keep up with breaking news and LinkedIn to network with clients and business leads.[32]

So how do companies use social media? That depends on the company's size and purpose. Mid-size businesses often use social media similarly to build a brand and attract new customers. In fact, social media use in the business world is expected to increase over the next few years, a fact on which aspiring leaders ought to capitalize. An article in *Marketing Charts* is one of many resources that explain this outlook:

> One aspect where businesses plan to use social media to a greater degree in the near future is customer service. Some 3 in 5 respondents are currently using social for customer service, while two-thirds (67%) anticipate using it for this reason to a greater extent in the next three years. In fact, about 9 in 10 executives strongly (46%) or somewhat (43%) agree that social media will become the primary channel for customer service.[33]

If you are not already using social media for career purposes, this is an optimum time to start. Here are ways you can potentially advance in your current job or prepare for your next one:

- Offer to create, manage, or curate a company website or department webpage.

- Organize essential information for the public, which is a fantastic way to build your expertise while developing marketing and communication skills, both of which are highly prized by employers looking to hire leadership candidates. Taking the initiative in this duty will impress your employer with your proactive approach to the job.

- Volunteer to coordinate your company's current social media posts and curate appropriate information for inclusion. This would be a valuable learning experience as well as a helpful service to the organization.

- Set up a new social media account like Twitter or Tik Tok on behalf of your company, with their authorization, and link to industry colleagues.

When you volunteer to manage tasks like these, don't surrender too much of your after-work time, or the higher-ups may come to expect it. A few hours weekly should be adequate. In time, you may want to request a pay raise in compensation for your social media managerial duties. Adding this experience to your resume will enhance your credentials and establish you as a growing authority in social media representation for business and professional purposes.

What to Avoid on Work-Related Social Media

One of the risks of taking responsibility for your company's social media accounts is that you may inadvertently adopt a similar style of posting content as you do for your personal social media. While it's easy to differentiate the two in your mind by viewing the company media rightfully as a job-related function, you might unconsciously slide into a personal mode of posting that could lead to questionable posts. Here are a few reminders about what not to post unless otherwise directed by your supervisor:

- **Personal details, attitudes, and information.** The company's social media accounts should focus objectively on relevant public interests rather than the personal lives of employees. Some companies might encourage you to use an informal, first-person narrative for a business blog, but many will prefer you to maintain a casual but company-based perspective. Discuss the style sought by the company before you start writing social media posts, and ensure you understand what is wanted. You could submit a sample post for approval first.

- **Inappropriate jokes or comments.** Although certain public forums like late-night TV shows or talk radio disparagingly discuss individuals, businesses, or industries, avoid that approach, even in jest. Don't mock, criticize or condemn anything in the business world. Doing so would detract from your professionalism, integrity, and credibility and cast doubt over your employer.

- **Company privacy.** Trade secrets, pending patents, or products under development should not be referenced directly or indirectly in social media or online content. Check to see if you can incorporate recent company press releases to reframe permissible information for social media posts.

- **Badmouthing the competition.** Don't condemn

competitors or try to keep up if they are leading the industry. Focus on your organization's strengths and achievements as well as benefits to the clients and public.

You can infuse personality into your posts within acceptable limits. Be witty, smart, and funny while sharing valuable information. But always make your posts relevant to current or prospective customers and tailor content to attract and hold their interest.

Social media platforms like Facebook, LinkedIn, Pinterest, and Instagram welcome businesses to share their stories or demonstrate products. You can also use Twitter to keep contacts updated about company news with brief but informative tweets.

Keep Your Content Sharp and Customer-Specific

If you are new to the role of posting social media content from a professional standpoint, here are tips that may help:

- **Read social media posts by the competition to see what they are doing right.** You might want to modify your company's style to fit a niche similar to and complementary to these existing styles. Check out what less effective competitors are doing. What makes them unconvincing or uninteresting?

- **Notice the format of the more appealing social media posts.** Are they short, long, wordy, or simplistic? While there is not just one right or best way to write social media posts, you can get ideas by examining those you find attractive or appealing that have large numbers of followers.

- **Decide whether to include photos, memes, or other graphic images.** These can work in a casual style on occasion but avoid overdependency on fillers. Keep the focus on strong written content to inform and persuade viewers.

- **Read comments posted by viewers to competitors' blogs and analyze their responses.** Consider how they might respond to your social media posts compared to those you are exploring.

- **Proofread each social media post before publishing it.** Grammar, punctuation, and spelling errors can reduce your credibility and cast doubt on your professionalism.

- **Get involved with other posts and with your viewers.** Leave friendly, supportive comments to others in your industry. Engage in a personable way with viewers who leave comments on your company's social media accounts. Use each comment to build rapport with the public to establish a professional digital presence.

As you can see, there are ways to get involved individually with your company, community, and industry to serve their interests as you build credentials and establish a credible public reputation. These stepping stones prepare you for managerial tasks and an eventual leadership position by enhancing your communication skills, connectivity to online and local businesses, and ability to become a company representative and professional expert.

Finding your place in the organization and establishing a niche based on communication and involvement will enable others to share ideas with you. They can learn to depend on your help and support when needed. In turn, you can build an extended network of business associates who may be able to assist you on your path to leadership.

Chapter 10

Step Up and Lead

When the call comes, will you be ready to step up to your moment to lead?

I hope you have found the information and suggestions in this book helpful in developing your leadership potential for future opportunities. Whether you apply for managerial employment or are tapped because of your abilities and skills, you will want to be ready to put your expertise to work when the time comes.

Sometimes the opportunity to lead arrives unexpectedly on your doorstep. A supervisor retires or relocates to another company. A new position opens in a branch office, or the company expands into a new region. Your cumulative experience and additional training may result in an invitation to apply for or be appointed to a leadership role. Often it is a matter of being available in the right place at the right time.

In this chapter, we examine the ways in which you may be able to lead from your current position in the company and your community. You may be able to find a niche where you can apply what you have learned about leadership. Initially, that may involve filling in for someone temporarily on leave or until a new person is hired. Let's look at options that could present you with the means to apply your leadership experience when called upon, which could eventually lead to a permanent or higher-level position.

Social Clubs: Giving and Receiving

In previous chapters, we discussed the possibility of serving in a volunteer position in a social context, for example, at church or in a hobby organization, such as a history group or a book club. Now let's consider how you can help others in need while utilizing your leadership knowledge to enhance your resume for win-win outcomes. If positions of interest aren't available, look for ways to offer your services.

Let's say your book club meets monthly to discuss a new bestseller. Your research has led you to locate several experts in your area. You consider whether one might be willing to give a talk at your club in exchange for the opportunity to sell their books afterward or for a modest speaking fee. You suggest the idea to the group, and they enthusiastically endorse it. Taking the lead, you arrange four speakers for the coming year, one every three months, to talk about their recently published books. You suggest that book club members organize refreshments based on each book's theme, such as tropical treats for a book set in the tropics.

You might propose establishing a small budget comprising donations by members to cover the speaker fees and refreshments. You set up a tentative schedule, make speaker arrangements, and organize a budget, all of which can become bullet points in your resume's leadership development skills while enhancing the enjoyable activities in your book club.

Now, if you take that a step further, you may want to combine a few local book clubs to engage a more renowned author to speak to the group. You enlarge your efforts accordingly, recruiting an assistant or two for help. Then you may want to take the group(s) to an area bookstore or a public library and invite the community. At this point, you are managing potentially dozens of club members, celebrity authors, and local businesses – all of which constitute an impressive range of leadership abilities.

Of course, you don't have to extend your club beyond a half-dozen members meeting in someone's living room with cookies and coffee. But doing anything further to broaden the group's interests or expand its reach can give you helpful experience in your leadership journey.

In her article titled "How to Improve Your Leadership Skills," in the February 14, 2022, issue of *Investopedia*, Alexandra Yan suggests that one of the simplest things you can do is use critical thinking skills and find ways to take the initiative to fix problems or improve the status quo.

> Good leaders are also aware of potential opportunities and take advantage of them to benefit the company and employees. In other words, be proactive. Don't wait for things to happen; instead, anticipate them...

Look and give thought to the social groups that are part of your life. Even if you don't receive official recognition or compensation for overseeing arrangements and developing new aspects of the organization, you are learning skills that can prepare you for advanced leadership of other entities. Here are potential outgrowths of exercising your initiative to enhance the activities of a group to which you belong:

- Your efforts may be recognized and celebrated on social media or the organization's media. The group may commend your work on their behalf by bestowing a gift or award that can be added to your resume.

- You might become the point of reference for creative endeavors when the group faces a problem or decides to grow.

- You could be asked to lead initiatives for growth or outreach or be recommended to hold office in the organization, such as president, vice president, or treasurer.

- If your group joins others or grows significantly, your title could become more expansive in overseeing a larger entity, such as regional director or activities coordinator.

- The group might recruit you to serve in a more visible or higher-level capacity.

Even if none of these things happen, you will have gained valuable insight into the managerial aspects of a local organization. You can add these experiences to your resume to demonstrate your willingness to serve where needed, confirm others' confidence in you, and reveal your ability to reap results. Your self-confidence will increase and prepare you to consider other leadership roles to which you might formerly have never given thought.

The amazing thing about offering service and support to entities in need is that you can enjoy benefits that bounce back to you from your assistance to others. It's a great feeling to help others and improve the quality of a program. Take inventory of your lifestyle to see if there are leadership needs you can fill. Even seemingly minor or inconsequential opportunities could provide the means to put into action what you have learned about taking responsibility and leading the way forward when others depend on you.

Community Service: Growth and Gain

Moving from a personal organization to a community-oriented entity, you can find plentiful information on how to become a leader. It starts with a vision of what you would like to see in your community. This may be to reduce crime at children's playgrounds, incorporate more green space in the industrial areas, or create a litter cleanup program for the business district.

Even if you lack the time or knowledge to launch an initiative of this type, you can join one that has already formed or suggest a group to a community council with the resources to act. You can attend planning meetings or share ideas with the group in charge. Whatever your involvement, you will learn more about the process of organizing a major improvement project, which will contribute to your managerial skills at the professional level.

An online resource called the Community Tool Box offers a valuable range of suggestions and resources. For example, when organizing a group of volunteers or workers to conduct a project, the resource recommends keeping the following in mind (listed here in part):

> **Think about the individuals in the group.** As a leader, you need to think about how each individual is affecting the group. Are there individuals whose talents are not being well used? Is someone acting in a way that is divisive or is draining the group of its energy? Is there a person who needs some help learning how to work in a team?
>
> **Think about the group as a whole.** Someone has to think about the group as a whole. Is the group cohesive?

Do people in the group have a shared vision? Is there trust and a sense of mutual support? Does the group need some training to help it function better? Are there some policies the group needs to strengthen it?

Get the work done. Someone has to wade through the mud and do whatever it takes. This includes getting others to help and making sure that all the bases are covered so that the job gets done right; when need be, it also means printing out labels, cleaning up the kitchen, making those extra phone calls, staying up late, or getting up very early.[34]

Here are the follow-up steps proposed by the Community Tool Box:

- Find people who have leadership potential. There are people all around you who would love to be invited to lead something.

- Help people view themselves as leaders. You can do this by helping them notice the informal leadership they have already taken in their lives. Are they parents? That is *certainly* a leadership position.

- Help people identify the reasons they want to lead. Listen to people talk about what is important to them and what they wish they could change.

- Assist people to choose leadership goals that are attainable, and that will help them build their confidence. Nothing succeeds like success.

- Support people while they work to reach their goals. Listen to them talk about their successes and their feelings of discouragement; appreciate them and encourage them to keep going.

- Support people when they make mistakes. Everybody needs help when they make mistakes. Help them get on the right track and encourage them to stick with it.

- Challenge people to take the next step.[35]

You can see how these actions could easily translate into the workplace. When you put your heart into accomplishing something, you can often find people to help you get it done. The same principle applies at work. When you wholeheartedly apply yourself to managing a task, you will find people who support you and enlist others who are not immediately on board with your vision. Your apprenticeship-type experience will give you the tools to convince colleagues of the merit of your project and encourage them to get on board.

Community organizations typically have their own means of connecting to the public with announcements of an upcoming project, status updates, and public relations. These groups use the same advertising media as professional businesses: press releases, social media, organization newsletters, and flyers or posters. Your involvement in the project will be recognized at some level, even if it's just the organization's meeting minutes. You might be able to forge a link between your employer and the community group. You can share your achievements at work via the company newsletter or website if these include external activities of employees. You can also include your success in your personal social media, which usually does not go unnoticed by your colleagues and employer.

Directly or indirectly, your community support and involvement will be noticed – and it may help you be considered for job-related leadership projects.

Networking is another benefit of serving the local community. While serving community needs, you may have the chance to collaborate with other local leaders: council members, contractors, and business developers. Some may provide references for you on request, or they might recommend you for a position at companies where they work or have influence.

Company Needs: Temporary or Permanent

Maybe you have had little interest in leading others until recently. It's possible you decided over time that you have the interest and abilities to fill a leadership role. So far, you don't have all the qualifications, or a position that suits your skills has not yet opened so that you can apply for it. Don't wait for the perfect opportunity. Be available for short-term or minor managerial roles that will let your abilities shine through and pave the way to more substantial positions later.

Have you been asked to lead a meeting in the absence of a department head? It may not seem like a glamorous role. In fact, it might feel like one more burden to bear on the job. Whether it's a single meeting or several, consider it a building block in establishing your reputation as a leader.

A middle-aged man who held a mid-level managerial position was asked to cover for his supervisor when she went on maternity leave for several months. Reluctantly but good-naturedly, Jerry (not his real name) took over for his boss and did an excellent job. However, he took a no-frills approach while maintaining basic duties. When his boss returned to work, he eagerly stepped down and showed no further interest in managerial roles.

His coworker, Christa, worked for the same supervisor. When their boss took another leave two years later, Jerry politely declined to cover for her. Christa was asked to fill in during her boss's absence and happily accepted. She did such impressive work by initiating a new departmental record-keeping system and frequently assisting and encouraging coworkers that her boss gave her a glowing report when she returned. Subsequently, Christa was offered her boss's position when the supervisor resigned to raise her family. An external search to fill the position was not even executed. Everyone in the department praised Christa and wanted her to assume the permanent leadership role despite her limited leadership experience. Jerry didn't mind at all, as he did not want to assume higher-level responsibilities.

Whether caused by illness, resignation, or relocation, a leadership role can open anytime, often without much notice. You can prepare for these surprise opportunities by becoming familiar with the company's flowchart of responsibility to find out who is next in the line of succession and if they are likely to accept a leading role. You may get an idea of how good a fit they will be in that position. Meanwhile, you should continue honing your skills and preparing to take the reins if offered.

As Alexandra Yan states in her article, you can prepare for when such a time comes.

> By showing that you have what it takes to be a leader, you can fast-track your career. If you're looking for a new job or promotion, you're more likely to get where you want to go if you have a steady history of being successful in leadership roles in your professional and personal life.[36]

Leadership on the job involves a plethora of skills. To become a leader in a larger role than you hold now, you may need to work on new skills while refining existing abilities. Many career agencies and success coaches advocate for practicing the following:

- **Self-discipline.** Make the most of your current role and be persistent in following through on whatever you are assigned to do. Don't get careless in mundane tasks. Always do your best, as an ethical imperative, and remember that others will be watching.

- **Listening.** Pay attention to information coming from multiple sources at your workplace. The water cooler lets you know what's on your coworkers' minds. Committee meetings reveal where the company is headed. Customer feedback provides information on what is working and what is not. The more you can glean from observation, the more knowledge you will compile for your personal and professional growth.

- **Motivation.** Learn what motivates you. Discover what motivates others – your colleagues, team members, and customers – and provide it. Supporting others in their daily work while helping them develop improved skills will work to everyone's advantage and prepare you to play a more prominent role.

- **Conflict.** Every workplace has conflict to varying degrees. Different personalities, backgrounds, and objectives lead to opposing viewpoints and competing efforts. The key is to find ways to move forward and fulfill job obligations in a stellar manner to be ready when leadership knocks.

Here are expert recommendations to help you prepare:

- **Avoid conflict.** When possible, don't work with people you know are disruptive or with whom you often disagree. Politely request another job assignment or stay away from topics that cause tension with those individuals when you must work closely with them.

- **Mitigate stressors.** Organize meetings and projects to minimize issues that stir controversy. For example, if you know that a marketing colleague fiercely opposes using social media for business promotion, ask someone else to oversee it or try working around that option.

- **Emphasize others' strengths.** Instead of handling or micromanaging all the duties, play to coworkers' proven abilities. "With your history in B2B interactions, would you please oversee that aspect of our new product promotion?" You don't need to mention that this individual's customer interactions are weak.

- **Share the load.** Give everyone a fair amount of work when coordinating team projects. Don't play favorites or hold grudges against someone who has treated you unfairly. Establish a track record of ethical consideration and mutual respect.

Putting your best foot forward will not only prepare you for a future leadership role but also help you build trust and mentor others who are climbing the ladder behind you.

Learning how to guide and direct coworkers is another skill required in leadership positions. The ability to have a good relationship with others and be supportive of their growth will designate you as a caring leader whose achievements will multiply by influencing others.

Closing Thoughts

There is a lot to absorb from the ten chapters in this book. I have included ideas and resources that have helped me and people I know cultivate leadership potential. I love my job, helping others do their best work in service to our employer and our customers while continuing to thrive and grow. Leadership is a lifelong journey on a path where you continue to learn. You should continue reading books by knowledgeable authors, listening to motivational speakers, and helping coworkers achieve their potential. All these will help your inner qualities blossom and produce fruit in your professional life.

You have discerned by now that the core message I want to share with you is to look deep within yourself to find undiscovered talents that can help you become the person you want to be. Are leaders born, or are they made? I believe anyone can become a leader if they believe in themselves and do what it takes to cultivate their innate abilities. All the strategies in this book are free or affordable. They are convenient and can be fitted into most schedules. If you want to or have been called to lead, adopt the suggestions in these pages as you step up to take the reins.

You may not yet know everything about leadership. Use what you have and continue to learn through daily observations and interactions. Gain additional experience when feasible. As your leadership focus sharpens, you can more efficiently prepare to influence others using the style best suited for your personality. With time, patience, and persistence, you will become an even more effective leader. When your moment to lead comes, you will be ready to shine.

———

If you would like to contact Jacob Isaac, please email jakeisaacdaily@gmail.com

Endnotes

1. Jenna (Britton) Arak, "6 Ways Keeping a Journal Can Help You Career," *The Muse*, June 19, 2020, www.themuse.com/advice/6-ways-keeping-a-journal-can-help-your-career

2. Olga Rogacka, "12 Stories from Leaders: Their Mistakes and Lessons Learned," *Success*, August 27, 2020, www.livechat.com/success/stories-from-leaders-mistakes-lessons-learned/

3. Roberta Matuson, "Evergreen Leadership Lessons from the Ever Given Fiasco," LinkedIn, April 6, 2021, linkedin.com/pulse/evergreen-leadership-lessons-from-ever-given-fiasco-roberta-matuson/

4. Jim Rohn, "The Power of Sharing What You Know," *Success*, March 6, 2016, www.success.com/rohn-the-power-of-sharing-what-you-know

5. *The Amplified Bible*, The Lockman Foundation, 1954, 1958, 1962, 1964, 1965, 1987

6. Kay Peterson, "Leaders, Learn How to Lead," *Forbes*, February 25, 2019, www.forbes.com/sites/forbescoachescouncil/2019/02/25/leaders-learn-how-to-learn/

7. Ibid.

8. Marissa Levin, "Reading Habits of the Most Successful Leaders That Can Change Your Life Too," *Inc.com*, August 13, 2017, www.inc-aus.com/marissa-levin/reading-habits-of-the-most-successful-leaders-that.html

9. Ed Fernyhough, "How Reading Changes Your Brain," *The Brave Writer*, January 8, 2021, medium.com/the-brave-writer/how-reading-changes-your-brain-b00cc7f8eb2c

10. Lauren A. Keating, Peter A. Heslin, and Susan (Sue) Ashford, "Good Leaders Are Good Learners," *Harvard Business Review*, August 10, 2017, hbr.org/2017/08/good-leaders-are-good-learners

11. Brian Rashid, "3 Reasons All Great Leaders Have Mentors (and Mentees)," *Forbes*, May 2, 2017, www.forbes.com/sites/brianrashid/2017/05/02/3-reasons-all-great-leaders-have-mentors-and-mentees/

12. Marissa Levin, "5 Steps to an Effective Accountability Partnership, and 2 Things to Never Do," *Inc.com*, 9 January, 2018, www.inc-aus.com/marissa-levin/5-ways-to-make-your-accountability-partnership-work-2-ways-to-ruin-it.html

13. "Fact Sheet: Focusing Higher Education on Student Success," National Center on Safe Supportive Learning Environments, July 27, 2015, safesupportivelearning.ed.gov/resources/fact-sheet-focusing-higher-education-student-success

14. Susan M. Heathfield, "How to Deal With Difficult People at Work," *The Balance Careers*, July 25, 2019, www.thebalancemoney.com/how-to-deal-with-difficult-people-at-work-1919377

15. Susan Madsen, "The Key to Leadership Development Is Critical Reflection," *Forbes*, May 26, 2020, www.forbes.com/sites/forbescoachescouncil/2020/05/26/the-key-to-leadership-development-is-critical-reflection/

16. Catharine Ducharme, "Leadership Starts with Self-Reflection," LinkedIn, May 11, 2021, www.linkedin.com/pulse/leadership-starts-self-reflection-catherine-ducharme-clc-acc/

17. Robyn Whalen, "7 Tips for Promoting Positivity in Your Workplace," *Total Wellness*, February 9, 2017, info.totalwellnesshealth.com/blog/7-tips-for-promoting-positivity-in-your-workplace

18. J. Ibeh Agbanyim, "Smiling: Why It's Important in Your Personal Life and Workplace," *Psychology Today*, November 25, 2021, www.psychologytoday.com/nz/blog/humanizing-the-world-work/202111/smiling-why-it-s-important-in-your-personal-life-and-workplace

19. Ryan Holmes, "What Research Tells Us About When (and When Not) to Smile at Work," *Inc.com*, 18 November 2019, www.inc.com

20. Susanne Ricee, "What is Inclusivity," *Diversity for Social Impact*, February 29, 2017, diversity.social/inclusivity/

21. Bryan Robinson, "New Study Shows A Lack Of Trust Between Employees And Employers," *Forbes*, September 5, 2021, www.forbes.com/sites/bryanrobinson/2021/09/05/new-study-shows-a-lack-of-trust-between-employees-and-employers/

22. Ibid.

23. Kelly Greenwood and Natasha Krol, "8 Ways Managers Can Support Employees' Health," *Harvard Business Review*, August 7, 2020, hbr.org/2020/08/8-ways-managers-can-support-employees-mental-health

24. Hallie Crawford, "How to Achieve Integrity in the Workplace," *US News/Money*, July 31, 2020, money.usnews.com/money/blogs/outside-voices-careers/articles/how-to-achieve-integrity-in-the-workplace

25. "Professionalism at Work," Resume.com, January 23, 2020, www.resume.com/career-advice/career-development/professionalism-at-work/#:~:text=Professionalism%20is%20how%20you%20display,manner%20while%20on%20the%20job.

26. Jennifer Herrity, "Guide to Professionalism in the Workplace," Indeed.com, December 4, 2021, www.indeed.com/career-advice/career-development/the-ultimate-guide-to-professionalism

27. Patrick Bosworth, "The Power of Good Communication in the Workplace," *Leadership Choice*, leadershipchoice.com/power-good-communication-workplace/

28. Jamie Birt, "24 Reasons Why Mentorship Is Important for Mentee and Mentor," Indeed.com, August 31, 2022, www.indeed.com/career-advice/career-development/why-is-a-mentor-important

29. Marlo Oster, "How to build a culture of accountability in the workplace," *Workpatterns*, January 14, 2021, www.workpatterns.com/articles/accountability-in-the-workplace

30. Matt McLaughlin, "How to Run an Accountability Group," Elustra Consulting, August 14, 2019, www.elustraconsulting.com/how-to-run-an-accountability-group/

31. Landry L. Lockett and Barry Boyd, "Enhancing Leadership Skills in Volunteers," *The Journal of Leadership Education* 11(1) (2012): 233-244.

32. Gary Henderson, "How To Use Social Media For Business," *Digital Marketing*, May 11, 2020, www.digitalmarketing.org/blog/how-to-use-social-media-for-business

33. "How Are Businesses Using Social Media?" *Marketing Charts*, May 10, 2021, www.marketingcharts.com/digital/social-media-117074

34. "Chapter 14. Core Functions in Leadership," *Community Tool Box*, ctb.ku.edu/en/table-of-contents/leadership/leadership-functions

35. Ibid.

36. Alexandra Yan, "How to Improve Your Leadership Skills," *Investopedia*, February 14, 2022, www.investopedia.com/articles/pf/12/leadership-skils.asp

About the Author

Born in South Africa, Jacob Isaac was the co-founder and lead pastor of Calvary Ministries in Durban. He now lives in New Zealand and has held various leadership positions within the health sector, retail and in manufacturing.

Over the years he has led a number of multiracial and multicultural teams. As well as acting as a life coach and motivational speaker, he serves on the leadership board of Calvary Apostolic International Ministries, with a focus on prophecy teaching and leadership.

He is also the author of *Hope Rising*, and recently founded Kingdom Advocates.

www.ingramcontent.com/pod-product-compliance
Lightning Source LLC
Chambersburg PA
CBHW062035290426
44109CB00026B/2631